THE CAVALRY CHARGES

THE CAVALRY CHARGES

WRITINGS ON BOOKS, FILM, AND MUSIC

REVISED EDITION

BARRY GIFFORD

UNIVERSITY PRESS OF MISSISSIPPI / JACKSON

The University Press of Mississippi is the scholarly publishing agency of the
Mississippi Institutions of Higher Learning: Alcorn State University, Delta State
University, Jackson State University, Mississippi State University, Mississippi
University for Women, Mississippi Valley State University, University of
Mississippi, and University of Southern Mississippi.

www.upress.state.ms.us

The University Press of Mississippi is a
member of the Association of University Presses.

"Sailor and Lula and the Capital R" was originally commissioned by the
Los Angeles County Museum of Art for the series Cell Phone Stories to
accompany the exhibition of Andy Warhol's "Black and White Disaster."
The characters Sailor and Lula were depicted in director David Lynch's
film *Wild at Heart*, which was based on Barry Gifford's novel.

Cover design by Barry Gifford of his great-grandfather,
Boris Kruschevsky, in Constantinople, Turkey, circa 1889

Copyright © 2019 by University Press of Mississippi
All rights reserved

First printing 2019
∞

Library of Congress Cataloging-in-Publication Data

Names: Gifford, Barry, 1946–
Title: The cavalry charges : writings on books, film, and music / Barry Gifford.
Description: University Press of Mississippi : Jackson, [2019] | "First printing 2019."
| "Original date published: 2007." | Includes bibliographical references.
Identifiers: LCCN 2019008120| ISBN 9781496824387 (cloth : alk. paper) | ISBN
9781496824271 (pbk.: alk. paper) | ISBN 9781496824288 (epub single) | ISBN
9781496824295 (epub institional)
Subjects: LCSH: Gifford, Barry, 1946- | American essays—20th century.
Classification: LCC PS3557.I283 C38 2019 | DDC 813/.54—dc23
LC record available at https://lccn.loc.gov/2019008120

British Library Cataloging-in-Publication Data available

THIS BOOK IS FOR
MATT DILLON AND AMY TRIPODI

"*Serás lo que debes ser, y si no, no serás nada.*" ("You must be what you ought to be, and if not, you will be nothing at all.")

—General José de San Martín,
liberator of Argentina

CONTENTS

xi   Acknowledgments
xiii   Author's Note

BOOKS

3   B. Traven: The Man Who Never Forgot
13   Michael Swindle's *Slouching towards Birmingham*
15   The Thrill of a Writer's Lifetime
21   The Strangest One of All
25   Nothin' Good Ever Happens in Texas
29   Adiós to the Gaviero: An Encomium for Mutis
31   Black Wings Had His Angel
37   Notes on Neihardt
41   Read 'Em and Weep: My Favorite Novels

FILM AND TELEVISION

111   The Cavalry Charges
117   A Brief Dossier on *One-Eyed Jacks*
137   In Search of the City of Ghosts

145	Fuzzy Sandwiches, or There is No Speed Limit on the Lost Highway
149	Keeper of the Cat People: A Paean to Val Lewton
155	Confidential as a Baby's Cry
161	Souvenir of Evil
165	Sailor & Lula and the Capital R.

MUSIC

171	The Last Time I Saw Artie
175	Lost Interlude
181	*Madrugada*: Not Opera—Action Musical!
189	*Madrugada*: The Libretto

ACKNOWLEDGMENTS

These writings originally appeared, several in different form, in the following publications: Positif (Paris), El País (Madrid), Letras Libres (Mexico City), the New York Times, San Francisco Chronicle, San Jose Mercury-News, San Francisco Magazine, Beat Scene (UK), La Nouvelle Revue Française (Paris), Slouching towards Birmingham (Berkeley), Brando Rides Alone (North York), Texas Stories (Chronicle Books, San Francisco), the Nob Hill Gazette, Canongate Books (Edinburgh), Read 'Em and Weep: My Favorite Novels (Diesel Books, Oakland/Malibu), New York Review Books, the Guardian (London), Brick (Toronto), and Première (Paris).

The author wishes to express his gratitude to both Richard Grossinger of North Atlantic Books and John Evans of Diesel Boks for their permission to include essays from Brando Rides Alone and Read 'Em and Weep, respectively.

AUTHOR'S NOTE

"*C'est la grace miséricordieuse du destin.*" ("It is the merciful grace of fate.") Joseph Conrad wrote this (in French) in a letter to Henry James. Conrad went on to say, "It seems I am trying to tell you a dream." He was attempting to explain to his fellow writer why he wrote novels and stories. The writers, filmmakers, and composers whose works (including my own) are described in this book of (mostly) essays, understood that what Conrad defined was the driving force that drove them to produce in their individual disciplines those creations demanded by inspiration, resulting in merciful—if not always graceful—release. I recall the singer Joe Cocker confessing that if he had not been able to express himself as a performer, physical contortions included, he could easily have become a murderer. Hyperbole notwithstanding, Cocker believed it was the grace of fate that saved his soul.

BOOKS

B. Traven
The Man Who Never Forgot

Does it really matter who B. Traven was? Was he at one time a Polish locksmith named Feige? An actor turned radical journalist in Munich named Ret Marut? A German or even Norwegian immigrant to Mexico named Traven Torsvan? An American by way of Europe who at one time worked as a merchant seaman and disembarked in Tampico in 1924 never to set foot on a ship again? Or was he Hal Croves, in 1947 to present himself as the agent of the author of *The Treasure of the Sierra Madre* to director John Huston at the Hotel Reforma in Mexico City? Was he an illegitimate son of a German Jewish industrialist named Emil Rathenau and an actress named Josephine von Sternwaldt, or the illegitimate son of Kaiser Wilhelm and an actress named Helen Mareck or Helen Maret? Why did Ret Marut, anti-Semitic but rabid supporter of Jewish anarchist Gustav Landauer in Bavaria in 1919, whom many believe transformed himself into B. Traven, humanist novelist sequestered in Mexico after escaping from a death sentence for being an enemy of the state in Munich, attempting to flee to America and/or Canada, hiding out in Berlin for four years, making and selling rag dolls on the street with his paramour Irene Mermet—who later married a Columbia University professor/lawyer and lived in New York—spent three months in Brixton Prison in London for failing to register as an alien and who called himself Hermann Feige, have a hand-writing entirely different from that of a man self-credited with the authorship of a dozen or so novels plus short stories and at least one landmark work of nonfiction? The man called B. Traven repeatedly issued a statement that only the work matters, not the author, a conclusion with which I tend to agree. As Traven scholar Michael Baumann points out, we don't know anything, really, about Shakespeare or Homer, but their works are revered and studied endlessly. No, it doesn't matter who B. Traven was. What does matter—to me, anyway—is why.

Like many others, the first exposure I had to the works of Traven was through the movie *The Treasure of the Sierra Madre*, directed by John Huston and starring Humphrey Bogart, made in 1948. I never forgot the kid, played by Bobby Blake, selling a lottery ticket to Fred C. Dobbs, Bogart's character, in a Tampico cantina. Almost half a century later, Robert Blake played an unforgettable character called the Mystery Man in a film I cowrote with director David Lynch, *Lost Highway*. Little did I know in 1958, when I was eleven years old, watching Bogart splash water into the face of the kid trying to tell him he'd won the lottery, that it was the creator of their characters, a figment of a Dr. Mabuse–like mad genius's imagination, who was the real Mystery Man.

A few years after I first watched that movie, I began reading Traven's books. I read *Treasure* first, of course, then *The Death Ship*, *The Cotton-Pickers*, *The Bridge in the Jungle*, *March to the Monteria*, *Government*, and the rest of the "mahogany" series. I read his short stories in the books *The Night Visitor* and a little gem of a paperback I found in a used-book bin in Chicago that I bought for a nickel entitled *Stories by the Man Nobody Knows*. It was this book that made me wonder why: I didn't care so much who B. Traven was, I just wanted to know why he didn't want people to know.

The French symbolist poet Arthur Rimbaud stopped writing poems when he was nineteen, after he was shot in the wrist in a Brussels hotel room by his lover, a married man, the poet Paul Verlaine. Rimbaud joined the Dutch Navy, from which he immediately deserted. Throughout his relatively brief life thereafter—he died at thirty-seven—Rimbaud was paranoid that the Dutch authorities were in pursuit, determined to arrest and imprison him. Perhaps this is one reason why he fled Europe and the literary life and established himself as a gunrunner and slave trader for King Menelik in Abyssinia, the land of men with tails and striped faces. Rimbaud went south forty years or so before the man called Traven did. The difference is Arthur at that point stopped publishing, and Traven began. If Traven was really Ret Marut, fugitive from Germany, perhaps he carried the same fear, that of being apprehended and dealt with by the Old World authorities. What could be a better solution than to change your name, your geography, even your handwriting? (The handwriting samples made available by Traven biographers Karl Guthke and Baumann seem to my untrained eye to be initially masculine [Marut] and then feminine [Traven]. The latter's letters were probably written by Irene Mermet, who visited Marut/Traven in Mexico during his first years there. By the early 1930s, Traven's letters were written entirely on a typewriter and occasionally endorsed by only a sketchy, illegible signature.)

The question that is repeatedly pondered regarding B. Traven is: who really wrote these books? Did Marut—which name was undoubtedly a *nom de plume de guerre*—befriend in the Mexican state of Tamaulipas, where he lived upon arrival, another person who had already written or was writing them? I don't think so. I think that *The Death Ship* (published in 1926 in Germany, as were all of the other Traven books), was written by that renegade in German and badly translated by him into English in an attempt to make people believe it was composed by an American. Bernard Smith, an editor for the New York publishing firm Alfred A. Knopf, which published *The Death Ship*, admitted that he revised the novel extensively in an attempt to render the English palatable. Marut/Feige/Rathenau/Wilhelm/whoever then proceeded to glean stories from his new land, which resulted in the series of books concerning the peasant workers and their exploitation by the landowners in the cotton fields, oil fields, and forests. *The Cotton-Pickers* was originally titled

Der Wobbly, after the short-lived International Workers of the World, who were dubbed Wobblies; and the subject matter was right up Ret Marut's alley. The fact that this writer peppered *The Death Ship* with anti-Semitic slurs and insinuations, and later, in 1933, in letters to his German publisher, vilified them as "filthy Jews," "Jewified and Semiticized, front and rear," "greedy, slimy, stinking [in order to save your] Semitic department store business," etc., doesn't surprise me. Anti-Semitism, even in a so-called radical anarchist person such as Marut, and despite his support of Landauer, was deeply ingrained in him as a German. I don't see it as an inconsistency, I believe it as a cultural sickness, a disease as prevalent today as yesterday. B. Traven in his writings, at least until 1940, when he for all intents and purposes ceased publishing, championed the rights of the fellahin, the underclass, the *pobrecitos*, while at the same time painting them as noble, becoming a kind of modern-day mythmaker, consistent with his zealous, self-serving intellectual idealism. Who cares? He knew how to tell a good story and that's what counts. That's why his books became best sellers all over the world, even though they were ungainly, syntactically confusing, half-cocked, poorly translated or written. B. Traven, whoever he was—not unlike Joseph Conrad, who wrote his stories in his *fourth* language, thereby creating a unique style—had something important to say. He did not pick at inconsequential scabs, the way most modern fiction writers do. That is one reason why his work will live as long as there are readers.

In April 2004 I was invited to lunch by one of Traven's stepdaughters, Malú Montes de Oca de Heyman, and her husband, Tim, a British banker and writer, at their home in Mexico City. This had been arranged by a publisher in Mexico City who knew of my abiding interest in Traven's books, and who knew that I had, in the early 1970s, corresponded with Rosa Elena Luján, Traven's widow (he died in 1969) and Malú's mother. I had somehow obtained the widow's address and written to her because there was one Traven novel I had never been able to find, *Trozas* (*The Logs*), and I wondered if she knew how I could locate a copy. Rosa Elena generously sent me a copy in German, as there was then no English-language edition. I told this to Malú, who informed me that her mother—still alive but quite ill—had obviously recognized my interest as being sincere and sent me the novel as part of her ongoing dedication to her husband's work.

I also told Malú that in 1978, when I was in Mérida, in Yucatán, I met a bookstore owner who told me he had been to school in Mexico City with her and her sister, Elena, and who said he had met her stepfather on many occasions. He described to me the third floor of their house on The Calle Rio Mississippi, Traven's studio, which he called the Bridge, as on a ship, and told me that Traven, whom he addressed as Señor Traven, not Croves, had been unfailingly generous to him with advice to a fledgling writer. Malú explained to me that her stepfather used the name Hal Croves both in public and for his screenplays, in order to distinguish that body of work from the novels.

(Among his screenwriting credits were *Macario* and *Rebellion of the Hanged*.)

Malú showed me Traven's typewriters, one of which, she said, an Underwood portable—manual, of course—was the one he had with him in the jungles of Chiapas. She also displayed his sombreros, including a pith helmet in which she had found several strands of Traven's hair. "If I can find something to match it with," Malú said, "I could do a DNA study in order to find out who he really was." The truth, she admitted, is that even she did not know the origin of the man she had considered her father since the age of ten or eleven. She and her sister had called him "The Skipper." "He had the strongest hands of any man I've ever known," she said.

Malú and Tim were gracious hosts, and they invited me to look over Traven's books—not only the various editions of his novels, but the books from his personal library, which interested me most. Some were in German, but the majority were in English, especially the fiction: Conrad, Conan Doyle, Wells. There were titles by Mencken and books on gold and mining, reference works he must have used while researching background for *The Treasure of the Sierra Madre*. In the late 1970s, while working as an editorial consultant for a publisher, I recommended they publish Traven's children's book, *The Creation of the Sun and the Moon*, which they did. It was a successful venture, and during the preparation I met Traven's main American publisher, Lawrence Hill. Malú had known Hill, too, and I told her that once when I was having lunch at the Players Club in New York with Larry he had said that perhaps even Traven didn't know who he really was. He meant that the man called Traven, or Torsvan, or Croves, did not know his true parentage, and that this had much to do with the obfuscation of identity. It was only on his deathbed that he apparently confessed to Rosa Elena that he had, in fact, been Ret Marut, and that she could now make this information public. My belief, I told Malú, is that Traven always knew who he was, who his parents were, where he was born. For so many years, like Rimbaud looking back over his shoulder for the Dutch Navy, he was burdened and bedeviled by a similar fear, unfounded or not; and after any true or imaginary danger had passed, so had his ability or need to change.

One thing that bothers me, however, is Traven's last, belated attempt to add to his literary legend by writing and publishing a final novel, *Aslan Norval*, in 1960, twenty years after the last of his mahogany, or jungle, novels. *Aslan Norval* was published, to my knowledge, in German only, never in English. Traven would, in 1960, have been, at the oldest (his birth date was given variously as 1882 or 1890) seventy-eight, and, as described by Rosa Elena Luján, he was a vital, mentally and physically strong man almost up to his death nine years later. *Aslan Norval* exhibited the old anti-Semitism expressed by Ret Marut in his 1919 Munich magazine *Der Ziegelbrenner*, and by B. Traven in letters to his German publishers in 1933.

This last novel was weak and consequently was virtually ignored and went untranslated. Why did he publish it? The reason is that Traven was a writer, and he had never stopped writing, if only mostly in his head, and he could not change. The final truth is that B. Traven never could forget who he was.

Michael Swindle's
Slouching towards Birmingham

A few months ago, Michael Swindle and I were sitting on the rooftop patio of the Hotel Isabel in the Centro Histórico of Mexico City knocking back shots of Cinco Estrellas and chasing it with Indios when it occurred to me that we had been running partners for going on fifteen years, an association that we should in all likelihood maintain until one or the other of us is forced to deal with the devil. "All the way, baby," is how Swindle puts it whenever we part, confirming the pact with *un gran abrazo y un beso*. Seated on spindly wooden chairs on the sunny rooftop in front of the open door of his twelve-dollar-a-day *cuarto* watching *Mamacita y sus hijas* hang wash, similar to the circumstances in which Kerouac wrote much of *Mexico City Blues* atop an apartment building on Calle Orizaba in the 1950s, I recalled the first time Michael and I met. He had come to interview me at my hotel in New Orleans for *Details* magazine. We hit it off and just kept on going, first in N.O.— where he lived and still does—and then on the road along the Gulf Coast through Mississippi—where he'd lived until he was six—to Alabama—where he'd been born and grown up, to Florida, where I'd spent a large portion of my childhood and adolescence. We wound up at the southernmost point of the United States, Key West, where I'd lived during the 1950s with my mother in the old Casa Marina hotel. One early morning there was a violent thunderstorm and Swindle hit the deck, haunted by heavy flashbacks of Viet Cong rockets shelling Red Beach during the Tet offensive in 1968. He was in the Marines then and it was now twenty years later, but certain experiences are always with us, and Michael has—despite having dwelled for decades in the Quartier Cinglant in the Land of La Bas—the memory of Funes.

One Saturday night at the Dew Drop Inn on Lasalle Street in New Orleans, Swindle was dancing with a three-hundred-pound woman named Regina to Too Short when our pal, Prince Vincenzu Duda (a fugitive refugee from the Bukovina), said to me, "Michael really has a talent for enjoying himself, doesn't he?" He does, and his talent does not end there. Whether he's whirling with a big-leg woman in the wee hours, hunting gators in Terrebonne Parish, wagering on fighting cocks in Sunset, Louisiana, or facing off with thuggish mobs in Port-au-Prince, Haiti, Swindle has one hand on the wheel and the other where nobody needs to know. What he wants you to know is contained in this book. Read it straight through—all the way, baby.

The Thrill of a Writer's Lifetime

I recently returned to Cuba for the first time in more than forty years, since I was a young boy. My mother and I spent most of our time in the early and mid-1950s in Key West and Miami, Florida, interspersed with frequent visits to Chicago, my father's headquarters and our alternate residence. My father stayed regularly at the Hotel Nacional in Havana, where he had business dealings; and for a time my mother kept a house at Varadero, on the beach near the DuPont estate, about two hours from the capital. I have a snapshot of myself playing on *la playa* at Varadero when I was three years old or so, and a great picture of my dad with his cronies at Oriente racetrack in Havana. After Castro took over, however, my family no longer spent time in Cuba. My father died in December 1958, in Chicago, and my mother, who lives in Phoenix, has never gone back to the island.

I was invited to participate in an international symposium sponsored by a Brazilian organization to talk about life and its risks. My qualifications for speaking on this subject, it was explained to me, were simply that I had lived my life as a writer, not ever taking an academic route but taking the chance that I could support myself and my family on the basis of my (mostly) literary efforts. I have been writing stories and poems since the age of eleven—when my mother and father and I were still visiting Cuba—and it is true that somehow I have been able to survive and provide for others by virtue of earnings derived from novels, screenplays, and journalism. I am now fifty-four years old, and I was told not long ago that only one percent of writers are able to support themselves solely by their writing. If this is true, I certainly must consider myself a lucky man, because writing has been my abiding passion for longer than the lifetimes of Kafka or Rimbaud.

It was in Cuba that something so exquisite occurred that I consider it to be one of the greatest thrills of my life. One afternoon I was taken with a few others on a private tour of the Cohiba cigar manufacturing plant in Siboney, a *barrio* of *La Habana*. While we were walking around the nineteenth-century mansion observing the workers sorting and culling and rolling tobacco leaves, I asked our guide if Cohiba still employed a *lector*, a person to read to them to help pass the time. The tradition of *lectores* dates back to mid-nineteenth-century Spain and continued thereafter in Cuba and then Key West and Tampa, Florida, which became the cigar-manufacturing capital of the United States after refugees of the Spanish-American War settled there. I began spending time in Tampa in 1959, after my Uncle Les, my mother's brother, moved there, and the old cigar factories were still operating, although by that time the readers had been replaced by radios and the rollers by machines.

Our guide at the Cohiba plant asked me if I wanted to meet their *lector*, and I said, "Of course." While we waited for her I thought about the history of these readers, who read everything from newspapers to Tolstoy, Dostoevsky, and potboilers. A large black woman named Zaida greeted me, introducing herself as *la lectora*. She asked me what my profession was and I explained that I was a novelist and screen-writer—"*Yo soy un escritor de las novelas y películas*"—and that I was pleased to learn that the tradition of the reader still existed in Cuba. Zaida asked me what I had written that she might have heard of. I told her that the most likely story of mine would be my novel *Wild at Heart*, in Spanish *Salvaje de corazón*, which had been made into a popular film. *La lectora*'s eyes lit up and she grabbed me and gave me *un gran beso* (a big kiss) and *un abrazo* (a hug). "*Salvaje de corazón* is one of my favorites!" she exclaimed. "I love *Salvaje de corazón*! Sailor *y* Lula!"

I assumed that she must have been referring to the movie rather than the novel—the Cubans lift American films off satellite and broadcast them on national television. It didn't matter to me, since I'm very fond of the film version.

I then mentioned to Zaida that my practice is to carry with me to foreign countries a copy of a book of mine in the language of that country whenever possible, to use as a kind of secondary identification in case I lose my money and passport; this way I can at least prove who I am—especially if there is a photograph of me on the book cover—and get someone to loan me money until I can wire for more. I happened to be carrying with me in my pack that day a paperback copy of *Salvaje de corazón*. I took it out and Zaida snatched it out of my hands. She kissed the front cover and insisted that I sign it for her, which I did. Zaida said that she read each day to the workers for an hour and a half, and that she was on the final chapter of a romance novel at the moment, but she promised that when she finished she would read *Salvaje de corazón* next. I told her I would be honored if she did this.

Zaida took my arm and proceeded to show me around, introducing me to her special friends among the workers, letting them know that I was the author of *Salvaje de corazón*, the next novel that she would be reading for them. As we passed from room to room, most decorated with photographs and portraits of Che Guevara and signs reading "*Seguimos en combat*" ("We are still in the fight") and "*Viva la revolución!*" Zaida handed me a selection of cigars, which I gratefully accepted.

Later, as my friend José Pinto and I were descending the steps of the Cohiba house, waving goodbye to Zaida and others, José, who lives in Madrid, said to me "My God, Barry, that was amazing. What a great coincidence that not only did she know your work but that you happened to have a copy of the book with you. What a thrill."

What had happened hadn't quite sunk in yet, but I acknowledged that this sort of unexpected event validated my efforts in a way I never could have imagined. I shivered a little in the heat. "José," I said, "what more could a writer ask for?"

The Strangest One of All

The first time I met William Burroughs was in 1975 at the Bunker, his windowless dwelling on the Bowery in New York City. Number 222, I believe, was the address, directly across the street from the Lighthouse Mission. It was from the Lighthouse Mission that I was instructed to call him from the pay phone so that he or his assistant could come down to the street-level entrance and unlock the accordion gate in order that I might enter William's inner sanctum. The Bunker was simply but tastefully furnished. I remember his telling me that at one time the space had been the boys' locker room of the neighborhood YMCA. Two or three of the stand-up urinals were still in place in the area partitioned off for use as a bathroom. Given William's particular affection for young men, what could have been more perfect?

I saw Burroughs again in the fall of that year in Boulder, Colorado, to which he had come to teach at the Jack Kerouac School of Disembodied Poetics. In 1981, Burroughs moved to Lawrence, Kansas, not very far from his Ladue, Missouri, birthplace, where he lived until his death in a modest wooden house on Learnard Street. I visited him several times during his residence in Lawrence, but it was in 1991, when my son, Buck, who was then sixteen years old, accompanied me, that was surely the most memorable visit.

Buck and I, accompanied by our friend Jimbo Carothers, a legendary retired baseball player from Kansas, spent a few hours with William on a hot August afternoon. Burroughs was then seventy-seven, and on our way over to his house I told Buck, who had no idea who William was, a bit of Burroughs's history. I informed Buck that he was a famous writer, a Harvard graduate, who had lived in Mexico, Morocco, England, France, New Orleans, Texas, and New York, among other places, worked as an exterminator and private detective, was heir to a family fortune and had been for many years—despite his frequent public denials—a remittance man, during much of which time he had been a drug addict (mainly heroin), had shot and killed by accident his wife while playing William Tell in Mexico City, had embraced and then rejected Scientology, had written several groundbreaking works of futuristic, satirical literary fiction, was now a painter of some merit, had acted in a few feature films, and had been for most of his life a confirmed pederast.

"What's that?" asked Buck. "What's a pederast?"

"A homosexual," I said.

"Oh. Okay," said Buck.

William, who had recently seen his novel *Naked Lunch* made into a film, asked me what I thought of the film version of my novel *Wild at Heart*, also a recent production, and showed us one of the "mug-wumps" used in *Naked Lunch* that he had chained to a chair in his painting studio. We had tea and he showed me the manuscript of a book he was working on about dreams. William steered the conversation to firearms, and pulled up his right pant leg to reveal an ankle holster fitted with a small-caliber revolver strapped to his skinny red- and blue-veined leg.

"I'm always armed," he said in his nasal whine. "In fact, I'm going out later to a place I have by a lake to shoot. If you like, you boys can come along."

Jimbo Carothers, who had driven us to Burroughs's house, explained that we had an early dinner engagement, so we would have to take a rain check on the shooting party.

William got up to get something in another room, and while he was out of earshot, Jimbo whispered to me, "I've done many crazy things in my time, but shooting guns with William Burroughs is not going to be one of them."

William came back with a large jar. He sat next to Buck on a small couch and showed it to him.

"Look at this," William said, "a brown recluse spider. Found him crawling along the windowsill in the bedroom."

Buck took the bottle and looked at the large spider.

"A bite from this spider will make a hole in a person's leg the size of a saucer," said William.

He got up and took a book off a shelf, sat down again next to Buck, and opened the book.

"Here's some pictures of spider bites. The brown recluse does the most damage," Burroughs said, smiling.

The graphic photographs of epidermal craters cause by arachnids clearly delighted him.

Later, William instructed Buck in the use of a blow-dart gun from New Guinea that he kept by his fireplace. He told Buck that the tips of the darts—they were shooting at a target nailed to the back of the front door—were dipped before hunting into a powerful poison that immobilized within a few seconds any beast so pierced.

"The hunter," Burroughs explained, "then takes a machete to the fallen prey and decapitates it."

Again, William smiled.

In the car on our way to Jimbo's house, Buck seemed particularly thoughtful and quiet. I asked him if he had enjoyed his visit with Burroughs.

"Yeah, sure," he said. "You know, Pop, you've introduced me to a lot of strange people, but I think that William Burroughs is the strangest one of all."

Nothin' Good Ever Happens in Texas

When I was a kid in Tampa, Florida, I once heard somebody say, "Nothin' good ever happens in Texas." I believe this was said upon hearing the news that a mad gunman named Charles Whitman had just shot and killed sixteen people and wounded a number of others from a tower on the campus of the University of Texas at Austin, before the cops put him down permanently. I know the implied admonition of that statement occurred to me when I learned that John F. Kennedy had been drilled in Dallas. Sure, terrible things happen in other places; Texas doesn't have a monopoly on violent or irrational behavior, but few areas seem to take such inordinate pride in bloody legends.

One of my favorite periods of Texas history is the time of the War Between the States, when Brownsville was seized from the Union forces by Colonel Rip Ford, a former captain of the Texas Rangers. Ford commanded a renegade army composed of young boys and men too old to have been conscripted into either the Union or

Confederate forces. The self-appointed colonel organized his minions using the canard that the federals were about to flood south Texas with Negro troops. Ford falsely claimed association with the Confederate Army, which operated out of Matamoros, across the Mexican border, but they distrusted him; with good reason, as it turned out, because as the war was winding down and defeat for the Confederacy seemed certain, Ford attempted to make a deal with the US government whereby Texas would rejoin the Union and his ragamuffin brigade would then join federal troops in a war on Mexico.

Fighting along the border was as ferocious and bloody as any in the rest of the country at that time. Ford's brigands managed to drive the Union boys into Mexico, where the United States was allied with the Juaristas in an effort to overthrow the Imperialists. Local border warlords—the Yellow Flags and the Red Flags—vied with bands of Kickapoo and Apache Indians for territory, as well as clashing with mercenary raiders such as Ford's bunch. Richard King and Mifflin Kenedy, Yankee businessmen who established the King Ranch in south Texas, had come down to profit in the steamboat trade. Rip Ford aided their betrayal of the Union by facilitating the rechartering of their boats under Mexican registry, which allowed them to transport cotton to the thousands of European ships waiting off Matamoros.

Just across the border on the Mexican side, at the end of what is now Texas Highway 4, lay the small town of

Boca del Rio, or, as the Europeans named it, Baghdad. Baghdad was a wide-open place where any kind of deal went down. People from all over came to get rich quick: whores, spies, gamblers, con men, army deserters swarmed in. Wages were high and life was cheap; there was no law. Baghdad was like Tangier when it was an international port. Mosquitoes, constant sand-filled winds, and murderous deviltry kept tension high. Almost immediately after the war ended, a hurricane destroyed Baghdad, cleansing it from the face of the earth.

It's this kind of past that Texans of my acquaintance seem to relish. Some of the contributors to the anthology *Texas Stories* (Chronicle Books, San Francisco, 1995), like Gloria Anzaldúa and Larry McMurtry (on occasion)—and some Texas writers who aren't included, such as Larry L. King and James Crumley—are also decidedly unsqueamish when it comes to Lone Star lore of blood and gore. One or two wax rhapsodic, but they're Yankees or worse—Jack Kerouac was from Massachusetts and Jan Morris is British. And Don DeLillo's brilliant reinvention of the myth of Lee Harvey Oswald (who was from New Orleans, more or less) gets Texas where it hurts.

I believe it was that venerable Texan J. Frank Dobie who paraphrased a Native American Coyote myth informing us that Coyote divided animal life into three categories: animals to be eaten, animals to aid in capturing food, and animals that would eat him. Man, Coyote taught, belongs in the third category. My guess is the man to whom Coyote was referring was a Texan.

Adiós to the Gaviero
An Encomium for Mutis

―――

Alvaro Mutis's Maqroll novels appeal to me on many levels, not the least of which is that although they are by definition fiction, there is nothing false in them. By his own admission, Mutis claimed that he never made notes or outlines for those stories, that he wrote only when the tales were ready in his head to be told. I feel a strong kinship to him in that my own Sailor and Lula novels (of which there are now eight) have been written in the same way. There is a spontaneity and verve present in the adventures of Maqroll that comfortably accommodates the erudition, eroticism, and wild, windy passages to and through a world nobody but a risky traveler like Mutis could concoct. Nothing is overprepared or stale here in this universe as hermetic as Faulkner's Yoknapatawpha. Maqroll the Gaviero, Ilona, Warda, Iturri, Abdul, Jamil and the others cannot escape "the intricate labyrinth of [Mutis's] irremediable odyssey" as their creator himself phrased it. My favorite of Mutis's stories is *La última escala del Tramp Steamer* [*The Tramp Steamer's Last Port of Call*], a great, even monumental love story told "with the slow, meticulous intensity of people who don't know what will happen tomorrow." Conrad, Dickens, García Márquez, even Poe, are present here, but only as observers nodding their approval. I didn't know Mutis, but I spoke to him once on the telephone when I was in Mexico City. He was near the end of his life and said he couldn't speak English anymore, so I forged ahead in my insufficient Spanish in order to hear the actual voice of the Gaviero himself, the lookout at the end of his voyage, knowing he was sailing in the Sea of Red toward the ocean of immortality. If this sounds grandiose, recall the last sentence of *Un bel morir*: "His wide-open eyes were fixed on that nothingness, immediate and anonymous, where the dead find the rest that was denied them during their wanderings when they were alive." I do not exaggerate when I say that in my estimation Mutis sits close to the head of the table in the pantheon of great writers of the twentieth or any century. I say close because I believe that Mutis would agree with me that the Old Testament of the King James Version of the Bible is the mother of all words, the windshield, and the rest of us scribblers merely bugs upon it. The rain comes, we get wiped away. But Mutis's words rained hard enough to leave a trace.

Black Wings Had His Angel

When I was the editor of Black Lizard Books between 1984 and 1989, the one novel I wanted most to publish in the series was Elliott Chaze's *Black Wings Has My Angel*. The book was brought to my attention by Edward Gorman and Max Collins, both of who had written admiringly about it. I read it and was floored. *Black Wings* was an astonishingly well-written literary novel that just happened to be about (or roundabout) a crime. It was a perfect fit for what the publisher and I were doing at Black Lizard, putting out books that were psychologically provocative, on the edge, and more often than not, over the edge. Our authors—among them Jim Thompson, Charles Willeford, David Goodis—were uncompromising, cruel, crazy, sexy, and daring. Chaze's novel, published originally in 1954 and since then widely available only in French translation, was to be a kind of crowning achievement for Black Lizard. Unfortunately, before we could publish it, the company was sold and the editors who inherited the series deemed *Black Wings* unworthy of publication.

As were many fiction writers of his era, Chaze was a disciple of Hemingway: brief, often blunt sentences devoid of unnecessary frills or explication. Like Hemingway, he was a newspaperman—the five Ws (who, what, where, when, why) were his commandment. James M. Cain, Paul Cain, W. R. Burnett, A. I. Bezzerides, and dozens of others rode similar rails, but what made these particular writers stand out was that they usually had a good story to tell.

I told many people about *Black Wings*, one of whom, the movie producer Monty Montgomery, paid Chaze a visit at his home in Hattiesburg, Mississippi, in 1987. Montgomery told Chaze he would like to consider making a film of the novel, but Chaze said he'd already sold the film rights to a French director/actor named Jean-Pierre Mocky, ending that conversation. (Mocky did, in fact, make a movie out of it, but not a very good one.) Montgomery told me that Chaze had been borderline polite to him, cordial but crusty.

It so happened that a year or so later, I was in the neighborhood (New Orleans), so I drove up to see Chaze myself. He and his wife lived in a small bungalow with a narrow porch out front near the railroad tracks. I knew he had worked for many years as a reporter for the Associated Press, in Louisiana and Colorado, and then at the *Hattiesburg American*, where he was city editor for more than a decade. He'd written a number of novels beside *Black Wings*, "literary" novels as well as a short series about a crime-detecting newsman named Kiel St. James. I'd found and read a few of these, and the only one I thought had anything to recommend it was *Tiger in the Honeysuckle*, a "straight" story dealing with racism. *Tiger* was all right, but nothing else Chaze wrote came anywhere close to what he had accomplished on all levels in *Black Wings*.

Chaze welcomed me warily, saying right off that in his opinion New Orleans was a cesspool of filth and degeneracy and that it literally stank. Why would I want to spend any time there? he asked rhetorically. Once inside the little house—his wife, Mary, he explained, was sick and locked in her bedroom—he took me into his study, sat down at his desk, and pointed to a gun in a holster hanging on a nail in the wall just above it.

"After my prostate surgery," Chaze said, "I was in so much pain, I came in here and took that pistol"—he stood up, removed the gun from its holster, and sat down again—"and put it in my mouth, like this." He put the tip of the business end to his lips, held it there for a few moments, then held it out away from him before resting his hand on the desk. "I decided to wait until the next day before I killed myself, to see if the pain slacked off any. It did, and even more the day after and the day after that. So, for better or worse, mostly worse, I'm still around."

Chaze was a fairly large man, seventy-two years old when I met him. He was cranky, bitter about having been mostly ignored as a serious writer but making attempts throughout our visit to pretend he didn't really care. He cared, all right; and his cynical façade faded the longer we spoke. He insisted on making us roast beef sandwiches on white bread with mayonnaise and the crusts cut off.

Chaze drank milk. When I told him I preferred to drink something else, he gave me a glass of tap water. We sat in the blue kitchen of his wooden bungalow and ate lunch.

Later we sat on the front porch and praised his magnolias that he pampered and that were growing all around us. I raised the subject of *Black Wings Has My Angel* and he said he didn't see why the hell not. I told him I'd talk to the publisher about it and that's how we left the matter. Chaze stood on the porch and watched me drive away. I had to make a U-turn at the corner and double back over the railroad tracks because the street dead-ended without warning. As I passed his house he yelled to me, "I could have told you to go the other way!" "Then why didn't you?" I shouted back. He smiled for the first time since I'd been there.

Two-and-a half years later I was back in New Orleans, picked up the paper one morning, and read Chaze's obituary. He had died without seeing his best book put back into print in his own country. I felt bad for him and silently cursed the new publisher who didn't realize what a little gem he had tossed away, thereby refusing Chaze the real pleasure he would have enjoyed at being rediscovered by a readership I'm very sure is still out there.

Now, thanks to New York Review Books, you've got the gem in your hands. Look it over carefully, it still sparkles. And on the horizon is the possibility that a new, American film version will be made. The producer Christopher Peditto obtained the rights and hired me to collaborate with him on the screenplay, which I've done. Billy Wilder would have been the ideal director for *Black Wings*; in fact, a crucial scene in both the novel and our screenplay echoes Wilder's *Ace in the Hole* (1951). But Wilder's dead and nobody makes movies like *Ace in the Hole* anymore. If this one gets the green light it's my hope that the film will honor both Wilder and, more importantly, Elliott Chaze, because nobody writes books like *Black Wings Has My Angel* anymore, either.

Notes on Neihardt

It was my good fortune to have been enrolled in a class called "Twilight of the Sioux" at the University of Missouri in 1964, taught by the Nebraska poet John Neihardt. I was seventeen years old and at Missouri to play baseball and football. "Twilight of the Sioux" was a one-unit course recommended by the athletic department to so-called scholar athletes because the instructor was well known for liberally handing out As, and was therefore a boon to shoring up athletes' grade point averages in order to keep them eligible to play.

I knew nothing about Neihardt, but I had spotted him on my first day on campus in Columbia, Missouri, a tiny old guy barely five feet tall, wearing a Homburg-style hat, wire-rim glasses, and a three-piece suit. He was bending down to sniff flowers growing alongside the sidewalks. This gentle-appearing little man seemed to me a curious figure, an anomaly among the fast-moving students and faculty members rushing around on their way to and from classes. Neihardt took his time, and I liked that.

In class, Neihardt spoke softly and with great passion and reverence for the Plains Indians: the Sioux, the

Cheyenne, and Arapaho. I was ignorant of his having authored *Black Elk Speaks*, basically a transcription of the words of an Ogala Sioux holy man, first published in 1932; it was on the Pine Ridge Reservation that the name Flaming Rainbow was bestowed upon Neihardt. In the late 1960s this book became a kind of sacred text for a new generation interested in Native American history and the notion of "getting back to the land." *Black Elk Speaks* continues to be a popular title to this day.

The other students in my class barely paid attention to Neihardt's lectures; they were there for the grade and were mostly biding their time until team practice. But I was fascinated by his narratives of having lived and moved among those last survivors of the ethnic cleansing perpetrated by predominantly white "settlers" and the United States Army operating according to the mandate of manifest destiny. Neihardt did not disparage this business of "civilizing" the West, but he did talk about the need to preserve the knowledge inherent in Native American cultures and to study their manners of survival. "Twilight of the Sioux" and *Black Elk Speaks* were inspired by Neihardt's interest in the Plains Indians' belief in the coming of a messiah to restore their lands to them during the mid-1880s, which resulted in what the US government deemed a rebellion that ended violently at Wounded Knee on December 29, 1890.

I left Missouri in early May of 1965, but I never forgot Neihardt. A few years later, I read his *A Cycle of the West*, five narrative poems originally published between 1915 and 1949; one of them, "The Song of the Indian Wars," he had read aloud in our class. I also read *When the Tree Flowered* (1951), a fictional biography of Eagle Voice, a Sioux Indian; *The River and I* (1938), a compilation of a series of articles Neihardt wrote for *Outing Magazine* in 1910 about a trip he made down the Missouri River in 1908; and, of course, *Black Elk Speaks*.

Neihardt chose to record many of his histories in the form of poetry, using a type of verse derided by the determined modernist Ezra Pound, who declared, in 1908 or so, that it was poetry such as John Neihardt's, celebrated by ladies' tearoom societies, that caused him to leave the country. Following his graduation from the University of Pennsylvania, Pound taught at Wabash College, a position from which he was fired for allowing a burlesque performer to sleep in his room—on the floor, he said. He embarked for Venice, Italy, and upon his arrival there proclaimed it, "a fine place to come to from Crawfordsville, Indiana."

Pound, of course, along with T. S. Eliot, William Carlos Williams, and James Joyce, among others, quickly eclipsed Neihardt and fellow practitioners whose work was favored by those gathering in tearooms; but it was the poetry and criticism of Eliot, before and after receiving his tutelage and guidance from Pound, that did much to establish, for better or worse, the foundation of English departments in American universities. It is unlikely that the poetry of John Neihardt is today considered an essential part of curriculum in literature classes.

I saw Neihardt being interviewed on television, in 1970, I believe, by the talk show host Dick Cavett. Like Neihardt, Cavett was a Nebraskan (though Neihardt was born in Illinois)—the interview took place in Lincoln—and Neihardt, who held the post of Poet Laureate of Nebraska from 1921 until his death in 1973 at the age of ninety-two, had become something of a mini-celebrity owing to the popularity of *Black Elk Speaks*. By then it had become a hippie handbook, outselling even Jack Kerouac's *On the Road*. I don't remember much about the interview other than that the old poet looked much the same as when I had encountered him in Columbia, Missouri, where he was still teaching and where he eventually died. I recall that Neihardt often wore a little flower freshly picked on his morning walk.

Ezra Pound was a great teacher, not only for T. S. Eliot but, through his books *The Spirit of Romance*, *Guide to Kulchur*, *The ABC of Reading*, the anthology *Confucius to Cummings*, and his *Cantos*, for me and by now tens of thousands of others. But so was John Neihardt, not as a great poet, perhaps, but as a personal historian of a time and place and culture that without his interest and diligence would certainly be less well understood and appreciated. What's more, I don't recall Neihardt ever having said a bad word about Ezra Pound.

Read 'Em and Weep
My Favorite Novels

For the Ideal Reader

Author's Preface

My friend Oscar Bucher suggested that I write these essays. He, as have others over the years, asked me to provide a reading list of novels that mean something special to me, those that had an effect on my life. Where to begin? In 1998, I was asked by the *Guardian* newspaper in London to provide a short essay for a series they were publishing called "I wish I'd written . . ." The first book that came to mind was *The Rose of Tibet*, an adventure novel I'd read when I was eighteen and have reread periodically ever since. I wrote about it for the *Guardian*, and the piece is included here. I did not make a case for this novel's being measured for greatness next to *War and Peace* or *A la recherche du temps perdu*, among others; my raison d'être for bringing *The Rose of Tibet* to readers' attention was to explain how it had inspired me at an impressionable age—as had, for example, Jack London's

Martin Eden—and whetted my appetite to take bigger and bigger bites out of the world. In one way or another, all of the novels (and collections of short stories) I've listed have similarly inspired me; and the great lesson to be learned from them is that the world bites back. In fact, it says here, you're bound to be bitten even if you never open your mouth.

As the man with the golden arm admonished, read 'em and weep.

—B.G.

P.S. After Oscar read these mini-essays, he told me, "I love it, it's not a reference book." "No," I replied, "it's irreferent!"

The Rose of Tibet
By Lionel Davidson

In 1965, I was eighteen years old and living in London when an acquaintance—whose name I've long since forgotten—handed me a battered paperback and said, "I think you'll like this." The title of the book—a novel—was *The Rose of Tibet*, the author Lionel Davidson. I hadn't heard of either and I asked the fellow who'd offered it why he thought it might appeal to me. "You seem an adventurous type," he said, "and this is a truly great adventure novel."

The Rose of Tibet is quite a bit more than that, a genuine work of literature. I was immediately charmed by the device Davidson employed to entice the reader into believing he's headed in one direction and then opening up an entirely unexpected can of bedazzling worms.

The story takes place in 1950, when the Chinese invaded Tibet, and details a man's search for his missing brother, one that leads him through a literally hallucinatory rite of passage. On this perilous sojourn he encounters a jewel of a goddess and a fabulous fortune, evades the predatory invaders, battles with bare hands an ursine monster in a blinding blizzard, and endures an erotic bout of nostalgia for a time that existed—perhaps—only in a demented dream; this last episode borne witness to by seventeen she-devil corpses.

I reread *The Rose of Tibet* every few years, and each time I am transfixed, transported. Among so many books, poems, and songs that I love, it's one work I wish I'd written. My old pal Ray in Brooklyn, New York, a Henry James scholar, told me not long ago, "You were right about *The Rose of Tibet*. It's one of only several novels to make a point of rereading on a regular basis." I gave a copy of Davidson's book to Ray thirty-two years ago.

The Rose of Tibet is also the one novel I'd really love to write the screenplay for. Whoever owns the film rights, please call me!

The Chip Hilton Novels
By Clair Bee

It was during the very early '60s that I discovered and read all of the Chip Hilton sports books by Clair Bee. The hero of *Touchdown Pass*, *Strike Three*, *Hoop Crazy*, *Pitchers' Duel*, *Dugout Jinx*, and twenty or more other titles, Chip Hilton, as invented by Bee, was a tall, handsome, blond-haired, gray-eyed boy in the small town of Valley Falls who was a great athlete and exemplary human being. There was nobody nicer or fairer or a more intense and dedicated athletic competitor than Chip, and I wanted to be just like him even though I had dark hair and blue eyes, wasn't particularly tall, lived in a big city, was not always nice or fair, and, even though I was a good athlete, was too often indifferent to the outcome of games in which I was playing.

Clair Bee had been a famous basketball coach at Long Island University, and the Chip Hilton series stressed sportsmanship combined with an acute knowledge of baseball, basketball, and football. Each story involved Chip in dual sporting and social dilemmas that inevitably culminated in a tension-filled but ultimately satisfying climax. There was never an unhappy ending. The overall title of Coach Bee's pantheon could just as well have been *The Gospel According to Chip Hilton*.

Chip lived with his mother, who was an operator at the Valley Falls telephone company. His father, "Big Chip," had been killed in an accident at the local pottery, where he had been foreman. My mother knew that I would have preferred her to be a little old gray-haired lady who worked at the phone company and did nothing else but keep house and care for me, and she used to tease me about it. She was a beautiful, sophisticated, relatively high-living young woman in those days, but I didn't really care because none of my friends' mothers were like Chip Hilton's mother, either.

Since none of my friends were any more like Chip than I was, I had a difficult time believing that somebody like Chip could really exist. Even at twelve or thirteen years old it seemed too fantastic to me—especially since the still-reigning conception of Chicago boyhood was James T. Farrell's *Studs Lonigan* (which I was also reading in those days)—but I still read each new Hilton story as it appeared. I was actually kind of glad there was nobody in real life—my life—like him. It somehow made the books more exciting, and at that point I had no great interest in reality anyway.

Years later I found the first three Chip Hilton books selling for forty cents each in a used bookshop in New Orleans. I bought them and reread the first, *Touchdown Pass*. Since it had been written in 1948, some of the football information was outdated, rules had changed, and certain strategies and formations were no longer employed, but the descriptions of the games still rang true, and though Chip was certainly as premier a do-gooder and as invincible an athlete as I remembered, I was astonished to discover just how right it all felt. There were good guys and bad guys and in-between guys, and though the story was a rather obvious morality lesson, it all seemed sensible without being overly righteous or hopelessly corny. I couldn't help thinking that if Somerset Maugham had written American boys' sports stories, they would have been something on the order of the Chip Hilton books.

In *Touchdown Pass*, Chip manages to help a friend's father find a job and get it back after he's lost it unfairly, captain and quarterback his high school team to the state championship despite a broken leg and keep the peace among warring teammates. All of this is accomplished while Chip holds down a part-time job as a storeroom clerk each evening and is an outstanding student during the day. Pretty Jack Armstrong–ish to be sure, but Clair Bee made Chip a bit different, he made him moody and often mistaken and even vain. That Chip was always able to overcome these lapses in character was certainly unreal, and rarely was a girl mentioned, but at least there was something real about him.

I imagine that I must have learned something from reading those books, and that I'm probably still operating according to some of those same principles and under those same delusions. What makes it possible to believe in something you know is impossible and to act as if it were not only possible but true? Maybe that's the only way anybody can ever really believe in anything.

Caution to Readers: Do *not* read the "revised" versions of these novels reprinted by a religious publisher. Find copies of the originals and read them.

The Man with the Golden Arm
By Nelson Algren

Growing up as I did in Chicago, Algren meant a lot to me. I began writing stories at the age of eleven, and I became aware of Nelson Algren's work around that time, 1957 or 1958. One of the first LPs I bought was the soundtrack from the film of *The Man with the Golden Arm*, with Shelley Manne pulverizing the skins Frank Sinatra faked as Frankie Machine. Manne, the Candoli brothers (Pete and Conte), and Shorty Rogers indelibly rendered Bernstein's score, a blast from nobody's past—the kind of sound that made me feel like there was a horsefly trapped inside my brain, frantically trying to escape.

Later, I read Algren's *Chicago: City on the Make*, a pithy, prole prose poem to a town that never really cared for its artists. Chicago was a no-man's-land for poets, despite the best efforts of Carl Sandburg and Eugene Field. Studs Terkel did what he could to convince the toughest audience this side of Buffalo that literature deserved at least as much attention as the White Sox or the Bears, but it was always a hard sell. Chicago was fondest of its hustlers and crooks, and Algren knew how to mythologize them. In the mid-'60s he appeared in Phil Kaufman's landmark Chicago film *Goldstein*, in which the writer tells the story of "Lostball Stahooska." This is Algren in his glory, a taproom poet who couldn't care less who his audience is as long as they keep a lid on it, nurse their short beers, and let him talk. I know he hung out for a while with Simone de Beauvoir and Jean-Paul Sartre, but I bet after a bit he felt like a pet coyote.

I never met Algren, but once, when I was in high school, I saw him on Roosevelt Road or Ogden Avenue, near the old Alex Club (where I learned to play the guitar by watching Magic Sam), going into a vacuum cleaner repair shop. I was with my buddy Big Frank, who said, "The place must be a cover for a fence. What would a guy like Algren do with a vacuum cleaner?"

Absalom, Absalom!
By William Faulkner

My former editor in France thinks this is the greatest American novel of the twentieth century. As it deals with race, our open, perpetually bleeding wound, and the failure of family, Faulkner couldn't miss hitting every reader where it hurts. It didn't hurt, though, that despite tipping his canoe over regularly into Lake Prolix, Mr. Bill was on late Saturday afternoon in midsummer sitting on the porch with a glass of good sour mash in your hand the best irascible big-ass writer of his day or any other. As Flannery O'Connor said when queried about comparing her own work to Faulkner's: "I know enough to get off the tracks when the Dixie Limited is coming through."

The Great Gatsby
By F. Scott Fitzgerald

I resisted this one for years, couldn't get past the first couple of chapters. Then one rainy day when I was sick in bed, I picked it off the shelf and saw what it was: perhaps the only almost-perfect novel ever written. Delicate thing, *Gatsby*. The rest of Fitzgerald's work, except for parts of his unfinished *Crack-Up*, never touched me. This book, along with *Absalom, Absalom!*, *Blood Meridian*, *Life on the Mississippi*, *The Long Goodbye*, and maybe *Martin Eden*, defines the American experience.

Blood Meridian
By Cormac McCarthy

This is McCarthy's masterpiece, not his florid, melodramatic *Border Trilogy* or the shadow-of-Faulkner-inhibited *Suttree*. It captures the Southwest in the way Virgil, Homer, or Shakespeare nailed their territories. Mythic, epic, fantastical, taking the Bible and the history books at their word, McCarthy created this stinking, ghastly, Beardsley-esque canvas to reveal us in all of our terribleness.

Life on the Mississippi
By Mark Twain

Orson Welles said that American literature began with the first 180 or however many pages of *Life on the Mississippi*. Ernest Hemingway said that American literature began with Twain's *Huckleberry Finn*. Jack Kerouac took Huck's tip and lit out for the territory. It's all the same: this is the riverbed.

The Long Goodbye
By Raymond Chandler

Chandler advised writers of fiction that, when in doubt about how to proceed, to have someone come through the door with a gun in their hand. I like almost all of Chandler's novels and many of his stories, but *The Long Goodbye* nails not only the LA of the 1940s and '50s but everything that came after and keeps coming. Duplicity never dies; instead, as Malthus postulated, it increases geometrically.

Martin Eden
By Jack London

This is the novel that made me believe in the possibility of being a writer. I didn't go to school to learn how to write, I went out into the world and listened and observed and worked and got beat up, and *Martin Eden* had more than a little to do with it. London's boy didn't figure things out any better than anyone else, and he didn't end up on top of the world, he ended up under it, but I understood the difficulties and the dangers because of this book and gave it a shot, anyway.

The Town and the City
By Jack Kerouac

JK's first novel and in many ways my favorite among his books. Sentimental, obviously derivative of Wolfe, Dreiser, Dos Passos, and others, nevertheless it tells a large American story about the disintegration of a small-town family, like a Frank Capra movie with a sad ending. Kerouac was already working in an autobiographical mode but invested much of himself in each of the characters that matter most. When I was living in Europe, I would sometimes get up in the middle of the night or in the very early morning and read parts of this book. It still makes me cry, for lost childhood, lost love, lost us. Alene Lee, upon whom the character of Mardou Fox was based in JK's novel *The Subterraneans*, told me on a windy, wintry day when we were walking together on Horatio Street in Chelsea, New York—it must have been 1975 or '76— that *The Town and the City* was the novel of Jack's she preferred. She said she thought it was honest.

The Neon Wilderness
By Nelson Algren

This collection of Algren's classic Chicago stories prompted Ernest Hemingway to call him "one of the two greatest writers in America." The other one, EH said, was Faulkner, but he was lying and everybody knew it, especially Hemingway. This is the best of Algren: "A Bottle of Milk for Mother," "The Face on the Barroom Floor," "How the Devil Came Down Division Street," etc. These slices of life from the West Side and in particular Madison Street defined what Herbert Huncke later called "Beat." Algren wrote these all in the 1930s and '40s and made him a kind of Bukowski-like darling of the

European intellectuals for a few minutes, seeing as how they liked to let the vomit and filth of drunks and bums sully a corner of their minds before going off to the Brasserie Lipp for lamb chops.

Sentimental Education
By Gustave Flaubert

Flaubert's fame relies primarily on his novel *Madame Bovary*—which is much better reading in French than in English—but *Sentimental Education* is superior. Frédéric Moreau's pursuit of the older, married Madame Arnoux is a cautionary history entirely devoid of sentimentality. A story told about Flaubert is that when he was working on a book and got a hard-on but didn't want to interrupt himself, he would masturbate at his writing table and then carry on. No mystery why he left frustrated Frédéric on the whorehouse steps.

Two Serious Ladies
By Jane Bowles

A seriously cracked modern classic. Boy, she may have been nutty, but Jane wrote rings around her famous husband, Paul. Mrs. Copperfield's Panamanian paramour, Pacifica, remains a recurring character in my dreams. I never get tired of her or this book.

The Death Ship
By B. Traven

Awkwardly written in any language, Traven's first published novel was and is an important statement on status and statelessness, to say nothing of the state of things. If William Burroughs said, "Anyone who holds a frying pan owns death," then in Traven's stead I'll say, "Whoever hasn't sailed on the *Yorikke* can't value life." A lesson in citizenship equaled only by the Marx Brothers in *Monkey Business*.

A Devil in Paradise
By Henry Miller

This is not a novel or, according to Miller, even fiction; but everything Miller wrote was blown onto the page by a gust of blarney. This one belongs in the category of the most unforgettable character I've ever met. It's a howling, horrific portrait of Conrad Moricand, a Parisian acquaintance of Miller's who later showed up at Henry's hideaway at Big Sur and became the man who came to much more than dinner. Never a fine craftsman, Miller lowered his verbosity level on this one because he finally had a lot to say about something—in this case, someone. Initially amused by the antics of his guest, eventually the gracious host hits the roof—literally! Moricand could have pissed off the High Lama in Shangri-la.

An Outcast of the Islands
By Joseph Conrad

The skipper's second novel, after *Almayer's Folly*, it's his first masterpiece. Can evil be bred by weakness? Can the world turn on a woman's expression? Ask da Vinci. Matt Dillon and I took inspiration from this story when we wrote the screenplay for *City of Ghosts*, and the great director Carol Reed made a damn fine film based on it. The ultimate take on the tropical lie. (No F intended.)

The Optimist's Daughter
By Eudora Welty

Arguably the most moving of Miss Welty's stories, this short novel is impeccably rendered. Death doesn't stop and, as David Bowie said, funny how secrets travel. If she hadn't been neurasthenic, Emily Dickinson might have written a book like this. A quality weepie. I've repeated this story told me by the Mississippi photographer D. Gorton before, but I like it so much here it is again: Gorton was making prints of Miss Welty's photographs for a limited-edition portfolio when one day she came to his studio in Jackson to look over the project. Miss Welty was then in her mid-eighties. She asked if she might have a drink of bourbon. "But Miss Welty," D. said, "it's ten o'clock in the morning." She nodded, seeming to recognize the impropriety of her request, then raised her eyebrows and lifted her right hand as if there were a glass in it. "Champagne?" she said.

A Good Man Is Hard to Find
By Flannery O'Connor

In a review of one of my novels in the *Chicago Tribune* a few years ago, the writer suggested (facetiously, I presume) that one late January or early February night in 1946 Jim Thompson and Flannery O'Connor hooked up and the result, on October 18 of that year, was me. If a certain sardonic humor that finds its voice in a kind of violent satire is an inheritable trait, then I guess the reviewer had a point. In any case, I took it as a compliment at the time.

O'Connor was much more successful with her short stories than she was with her novels, though they have their moments. *A Good Man* contains the best of the stories. When Ray Bradbury wrote, "Something wicked this way comes," he hadn't yet heard of Flannery O'Connor; but, futurist that he was, he definitely heard her coming.

A la recherche du temps perdu
By Marcel Proust

Along with *War and Peace, Ulysses, The Tale of Genji, Don Quixote*, and maybe *Finnegans Wake* (Joyce turns over happily in his grave knowing he's the only writer with two), *A la recherche du temps perdu* is one of the targets on the Big Novel Dartboard in the Sky. You can't say enough about this book, or too little, either. Proust was quite a character, as they say. Slept in a cork-lined room to keep dust to a minimum; always wore a heavy overcoat even in hot weather so as not to catch a chill. And then there are the rat stories, lately deemphasized by biographers Jean-Yves Tadié and Edmund White. According even to Proust's chauffeur, who claimed, "It was I who brought the rats to Monsieur Proust," the fey Marcel liked to observe rats being tortured with hatpins and straps. André Gide, who probably lied as well as any Frenchman, reported: "Proust explained to me his desire to conjoin the most disparate sensations and emotions for the purpose of orgasm. The pursuit of rats, among other devices, was to be justified in this intention . . ." Proust also invested financially in a boy whorehouse. If one goes by the logic that Pete Rose belongs in the baseball hall of fame by virtue only of his accomplishments on the field, that his gambling on the game is meaningless in the face of his 4,000+ base hits, then Proust is the cleanup man in the lineup of the all-time literary all-star team.

Dr. Sax

By Jack Kerouac

"Doctor Sax swept into the salon, his cape flowing and looping, his slouch hat half concealing a secret, malevolent leer . . . He was very tall . . . 'Transcendenta! Transcendenta! We shall dance a mad cadenza!'" JK's boyhood fantasy written on a rooftop in Mexico City in 1952. This is my pal Vinnie Deserio's favorite book of Kerouac's, the one Kerouac called "Faust Part Three," the dream of childhood revisited in the thrall of "The Shadow," when a voice in the dark from the radio made men and women shiver and children begin to understand the great snake of the world was sex and death and one terrible day even they would be swallowed and disappear.

The Short Stories of Ernest Hemingway

In the great grey moaning Marxist English departments of today, Hemingway's contribution to world literature has about been reduced to a couple of good short stories. The truth is that EH changed the way people write. He was so good, so early (and also so bad and self-parodying) that it's hard to believe. "The Killers," "Fifty Grand," "The Short Happy Life of Francis Macomber," most of the Nick Adams stories, and the perfect part of "My Old Man" when the kid goes with his crooked jockey father to St. Cloud and they get the tip on Kzar to lose is what

Mark Twain hoped would happen, that there would be an American Turgenev, and Hemingway was it.

War and Peace
By Leo Tolstoy

Tolstoy was able to translate his personal conflicts into art. A rich guy full of guilt and religious doubt, nasty by nature, trying to be and do good. He wrote a lot and it breaks your heart and you can feel the blood turn to ice in your boots. Take a weekend and read it straight through and then try to go to work on Monday morning without thinking the world belongs to no man.

Black Wings Has My Angel
By Elliott Chaze

I met Chaze at his house in Hattiesburg, Mississippi, in about 1989, when he was seventy-two. He took me into his study, sat down at his desk, and pointed to a gun-in-holster hanging on a nail in the wall just above it. "After my prostate surgery," he told me, "I was in so much pain, I came in here and took that pistol"—he stood up, removed the gun from its holster, and sat down again—"and put it in my mouth, like this." Chaze put the tip of the business end to his lips, held it there for a few moments, then held it out away from him before resting his hand on the desk.

"I decided to wait until the next day to kill myself, to see if the pain slacked off any." At this point in his story, I looked out the window and saw beautiful white, pink, and purple magnolias growing against the glass.

Red Harvest
By Dashiell Hammett

Not long after the film of *Wild at Heart* came out, David Lynch and I were asked if we wanted to collaborate on a movie based on *Red Harvest*. We met with the producer who owned the rights at a restaurant in Los Angeles. He gave me a script Bernardo Bertolucci had written when he was contemplating making it, which I later read. Bertolucci's screenplay had some great moments in it, like the part with underground fires bursting out, but it didn't capture the true hardness of the novel, the terrible behavior based on sadistic delight of the sociopathic maniacs vying for control of Personville (pronounced Poisonville by the inhabitants), which was based on the mining wars in Butte, Montana, that Hammett knew from his days as a Pinkerton op. Lynch and I never got the chance to make an attempt at capturing it because of some problems over the rights. None of this movie chat is important, but the book is.

My Name Is Aram
By William Saroyan

In the 1930s, Saroyan was the most famous writer in America, and these are his best stories. I knew Bill for the last few years of his life. He never stopped working. I once went into a tailor shop in Paris owned by an Armenian (Saroyan was an Armenian-American) and hanging just above the cash register was a portrait of Saroyan. At least the Armenians won't forget him.

The Short Stories of William Carlos Williams

Better known for his poetry, I always loved Williams's stories. He was a doctor and would scribble down thoughts, stories, and poems on prescription pads between appointments in his office in his house in Rutherford, New Jersey. He wrote a story about a good-looking woman in a gas station and I saw her red dress riding up on her rump, her long, slender stems and dainty ankles. She was chewing gum and I wished I could have told her to spit it out.

Victory
By Joseph Conrad

Conrad created the sexiest female characters of anyone other than James M. Cain, but they weren't for everyone, usually not even for his male characters who fell in love with them. Obsession portends destruction. If hell is for heroes, paradise is for the lonely and the lost.

The Short Stories of Henry James

Why the stories and not his novels? Because the short fiction of James so often frightened me. "The Beast in the Jungle," "The Real Thing," "The Turn of the Screw," and the rest—even, and especially, "The Aspern Papers"—are revealing of craven, selfish, foolish behavior made so revealingly and intelligently that when properly absorbed do more to addle and shock than any so-called horror story. I've always considered James, along with Oscar Wilde, one of the great, gruesome explorers of the mind. When I was a child and an adult instructed me to "be on your best behavior," I always braced myself for the worst.

The Short Stories of Anton Chekhov

Chekhov was a doctor who said, "I believe in the individual." The actors in his play *The Seagull* performed with their backs to the audience, whose reaction was so bad that Chekhov became suicidal. He and F. Scott Fitzgerald both died at the same age, forty-four. A crazy wife (or husband) will force you to figure out the game early, which is no guarantee of survival.

The Novels of Jean Rhys

There are only five: *Voyage in the Dark*, *Quartet* (originally titled *Postures*), *After Leaving Mr. Mackenzie*, *Good Morning, Midnight*, and *Wide Sargasso Sea*. The women's movement of the late '60s gave Rhys a vogue that she detested. She enjoyed dressing well, wearing makeup, and she was extremely vain; also, she was an alcoholic recluse. Nobody wrote more convincingly or skillfully about cruelty at the hands of others, one of the others being oneself. She was a much better writer than Ford Madox Ford, whose mistress she was for a while. The novels taught me the art of economy in language. Rhys cried victim but she did it so naturally you don't feel the razor cut until you see the blood.

The Adventures and Misadventures of Maqroll
By Álvaro Mutis

Maqroll the Gaviero (the Lookout, as on a ship) has a take on the world equal to Traven's Gales or London's

Burning Daylight, only he's an even greater adventurer. The several novellas (my favorite literary form) that comprise his legend as devised by the worldly and supremely clever Mutis describe a life for which there is no edge to go over; as the planet turns, Maqroll rolls with it, there's no shaking him loose, he's part of the fundament. My fondness for Maqroll begins with his profession as a sailor, a man who takes chances even with chances. Here you'll fall into an orbit as profound and magical as Marquez's Macondo, only you'll believe it really exists. Characters wilder and even more calculatingly insane than Trebitsch-Lincoln, Edmund Backhouse, and Baron Corvo thrive in these novellas, and Maqroll, always on the lookout, sees them for who and what they are but gets into bed with them anyway. After all, if you miss your ship, there's always another.

Nine Stories
By J. D. Salinger

Again, unease is the order of the day. More has been written—certainly more has been published—about Salinger's work than he has written or published. Salinger is the Big WASP of American literature (funny, because he's Jewish)—he delivers a sting so deeply that even after the stinger is removed you remember it forever. I dislike many of his characters, the way they talk, think, behave; others he idealizes and I love. He's puzzled, finally, so he withdrew and let the critics speak. Nobody will remember them.

The Short Stories of Guy de Maupassant

William Saroyan said "The Necklace" by Guy de Maupassant was the catalyst for his work. When I read the description of the young man relieving the lactating woman in the train compartment I was about fifteen and it's still the sexiest scene in my literary memory. De Maupassant is a touchstone for a multitude of fiction writers; we all owe him a great debt. He had his own style, his stories were accessible, and they made a point; he knew how to finish.

Undervalued as a craftsman. I believed all of his characters; he could have been a great screenwriter.

The Short Stories of Tennessee Williams

"The Mysteries of the Joy Rio," about the old pederast watchmaker and his young Latino apprentice in El Paso, Texas, is a story I reread with regularity. It's touching and beautiful and strange, just like the best of Williams. "Two on a Party" is also one I like to reread. Here's my funny little "connection" to Tennessee: in his play *Orpheus Descending*, the main character, Val, wears a snakeskin jacket. Marlon Brando played the role in the movie, retitled

The Fugitive Kind. In the film version of my novel *Wild at Heart*, Nicolas Cage, as the main character, Sailor Ripley, wears a snakeskin jacket "as a symbol of his independence and personal freedom." Nic himself created this affectation, not I or director David Lynch, as an homage to Brando's Val. Then Adrien Brody, acting in the film *Love the Hard Way*, which I titled and advised director Peter Sehr on, decided to wear a snakeskin jacket in homage to Nic Cage's Sailor. I have a feeling this reptilian replication isn't over yet.

Moby-Dick
By Herman Melville

A cornerstone of American literature, and at the very least, a doorstop. What would any of us have done without the white whale? You can read this as two entirely separate books: the story or the alternating chapters on the history of the whaling industry. I was always glad that Melville made the whale white, not black (because, of course, black is the shade identified with bad and white with good), but I would rather have had Moby Dick be gray. The great gray whale. Think about it. Ahab wears a black coat. The sea is blue, serene absent wind, whale and man. And now every person under the age of forty has a body marked up with more tattoos than Queequeg, meaningless and boring. *Moby-Dick* is neither.

Burning Daylight
By Jack London

"It was a quiet night in the Tivoli" is the opening line of this relatively obscure novel of London's. It's based on his gold mining exploits in the Yukon, completely over the top and redolent of his Übermensch fixation. Nietzsche with a dogsled. Burning Daylight (the wonderful name of the protagonist) makes his fortune, goes to the big city, gets cheated out of it by the financial barons, and after having gone to great lengths to civilize himself, resorts to brute force in order to rectify the situation. A wild, tough fantasy that should be the Bible of every survivalist on the planet. A gun, a dog, a cabin. Not a pretty picture of American womanhood, either. When Nietzsche took walks in the woods near his house in Sils, Switzerland, the local kids would follow and throw stones at him.

Of Time and the River
By Thomas Wolfe

The description of the train approaching the station to take Eugene Gant away from his boyhood North Carolina hometown forever is stirring, magnificent, sad, hopeful, poetic. Wolfe was so tall he wrote standing up on an upended steamer trunk, scribbling in longhand only a few words on each sheet of paper and tossing them down. He was huge and his novels were huge and you have to have a huge hunger to read them. Wolfe wrote a terrific short story, too: "Only the Dead Know Brooklyn." He was like Hack Wilson, the baseball player for the Cubs who hit 56 home runs one year and drove in 190, still a record. Wilson was a drunk and he didn't last long, either.

The Cotton-Pickers
By B. Traven

This is the first of Traven's Mexican novels, his Wobbly manifesto. The stranger, a foreigner, blows in (his name is Gales) and begins organizing the peons in the cotton fields. Traven himself had fled Germany, where he'd become an enemy of the state for writing and publishing a radical paper called *The Brickburner* under the nom de plume Ret Marut. Traven hopped a freighter to Tampico circa 1924 and for the rest of his life hid out in Mexico, but he couldn't keep his mouth shut. His cover was blown in 1948 when John Huston filmed Traven's novel *The Treasure of the Sierra Madre*. Traven showed up on the set and tried to pass himself off as an agent named Hal Croves, but Huston, Bogart, Tim Holt, and the cinematographer, Gabriel Figueroa, whose sister was a close friend of Traven's, knew better. *The Cotton-Pickers* sticks to the IWW line, but it's full of pithy witticisms and picks up steam as it goes along. Traven had just fallen in love with the myth of the fellahin, and so this is a kind of socialist social romance, if there could be such a thing. Call it *El marinero y los indios: un educación simpático.*

The Comedians
By Graham Greene

For the most part, I prefer Greene's "entertainments" such as *The Ministry of Fear* or *Stamboul Train* to his "serious" novels, but both *The Comedians*, which takes place in Haiti under Duvalier *père*, and *The Honorary Consul*, set in a fictional South American country, deliver the real goods, adventure and intrigue in a context that reveals the weakness and cowardice that underlies bravery in all men. Women, especially whores in rotting, pest-ridden outposts, seem for some reason to be judged by a different (or indifferent) God. God has much to do with Greene's work—he was a staunch Roman Catholic—and numerous opinionated sorts, such as Simone de Beauvoir, loathed him (but of course Sartre was her God and it got her through). My pal Mike Swindle stayed at the Olafsson Hotel when he was covering a coup in Haiti some years ago and told me it was just as Greene described it in his books. Swindle had the shit kicked out of him on the street in Port-au-Prince during a riot, but I'll bet Greene never did. He stayed cool and distant and lived in the south of France, one step above the fray. Remember that when you read him.

The Universal Baseball Association, Inc., J. Henry Waugh, Prop.
By Robert Coover

I haven't read this novel in a very long time, but I still remember it as the best real novel using baseball as a device, storyline, metaphor, etc. Coover early on proved he could stretch a double into a triple with one out (it's a cardinal sin to get thrown out at third with no outs or two) when he wrote not only this but *The Origin of the Brunists* (religious hysteria, coal mines), both books like Smokey Burgess, the great fat pinch hitter of the Pittsburgh Pirates of the 1950s; as an old-timer commented, "You could wake Smokey up on a January morning and he'd come up to the plate and line a frozen rope into the gap, then get back into bed and be asleep again before the pinch runner got loose."

The Killer Inside Me
By Jim Thompson

"If clichés could kill" could be the alternate title. Thompson wrote all the way through in this one. With some of his novels he hit a wall after sixty pages and limped home, but *Killer Inside* is a shit-storm of harm. I read it sitting at the soda fountain of River Grove Drugs in Tampa, Florida, when I was thirteen, most of it aloud to my friend

Vinnie Deserio, who said, "This Thompson sounds like our kind of guy." Both Vinnie and Thompson knew what they were talking about.

The Friends of Eddie Coyle
By George V. Higgins

Higgins was a Boston lawyer who listened to testimony from the types of lowlifes he featured in his best novels. I say "best novels" because his "straight" fiction (*Dreamland*, etc.) pales beside the crime novels he wrote, especially the early ones (*Eddie Coyle, The Digger's Game, Cogan's Trade, The Rat on Fire*). With *The Friends of Eddie Coyle*, Higgins established a new standard for perfect pitch, dialogue beyond doubt. Hammett created a model for this in *The Thin Man*, Nick and Nora nattering away wittily and intelligently. In the crime category, Elmore Leonard established a stylized if false patter that is always serviceable within the confines of his novels. In his recent novels—*Clockers, Freedomland, Samaritan*—Richard Price, also a terrific screenwriter, lives up to the standard set by Higgins. *Coyle* was made into a hard, lugubrious film by Peter Yates, most notable for the brutally beautiful interchanges between Robert Mitchum and Richard Jordan, two actors who knew how to play cool losers whose entire lives have been lived on the down-low.

Not Without Laughter
By Langston Hughes

A sweet tale, not a bit syrupy, about Hughes's childhood in Lawrence, Kansas, in the 1920s. And when the kid grows up and goes to Chicago, Hughes's description of Bronzeville, Black Chicago of the day, though it doesn't really square with the rest of the book, provides a picture of a time and place that could have been taken by Roy DeCarava with his camera. Years later, in Harlem, Hughes and DeCarava hooked up to create *The Sweet Flypaper of Life*, a photos-and-text portrait still lovely, timeless, poignant. Also see the collections of his Simple stories. Langston Hughes was a special case, a true poet without a bad bone in his body of work.

Don Bartolomeo and the Lariat
By Jaime de Angulo

De Angulo was a California anthropologist in the first half of the twentieth century who was a bane to academics. "Nobody wants an anthropologist who goes rolling drunk in ditches with the Indians," he said, or something close to it. He compiled the Achumawi dictionary while living in Modoc County. De Angulo, the son of a Spanish grandee, liked to dress up in women's clothing and go shopping in the market in Berkeley, where he lived before withdrawing from society to a ranch near Big

Sur. He drove over a cliff when he was drunk with his young son; the boy was killed, crushed against his father's chest, trapped there until rescuers could remove their bodies from the wreckage. De Angulo had to lie there at the bottom of a canyon, his dead child pinned to him. After this, he rode the borders of his ranch shooting at strangers. De Angulo wrote a series of Indian tales based on Native American myths, which became popular, but he also wrote short novels full of fire and madness that captivated me. He corresponded with Ezra Pound, who had the same kind of little beard and considered Jaime a genius. So do I.

The Grass Harp
By Truman Capote

The gentle side of Capote that includes "The Thanksgiving Visitor," "A Christmas Memory," and "One Christmas." I like these, along with his early short story "Children on Their Birthdays" and the terrifying "Master Misery." *In Cold Blood* and *Breakfast at Tiffany's* are other sides of the Capote coin worth reading, and *Tiffany's* is darker and tougher than the silly movie version. Little Truman had the mean reds, as he would say, every day of his little life.

Lost Illusions
By Honoré de Balzac

The novel begins with the history of the printing press and tells the story of a young poet, Lucien Chardon, who comes to Paris to make his mark. As I was a young poet at the time I first read *Lost Illusions*, come to London and Paris to discover what the world had to offer me and I it, Balzac's Big Ship sailed into port at precisely the right time. Thanks in part to Balzac's lesson, I managed to avoid the snares of Mme. de Bargeton and the Marquise d'Espard, only to entangle myself otherwise, but managed to avoid Chardon's fate of becoming a hack journalist. Balzac worked like a madman, he wrote hundreds of novels and stories; prose exploded from him like a volcano. Years ago, standing next to his grave at Père-Lachaise, I wrote in a poem, "He understood madness in men, as Zola, but Balzac couldn't stop to consider what might happen if he stopped / He had only fifty-one years / as if fifty more would have been enough."

Crime and Punishment
By Fyodor Dostoevsky

The first thing of Dostoevsky's I read was *Notes from Underground*, his missive of desperation, then *The Dead*, about his time in prison, and then *Crime and Punishment*. I was sitting at a window counter in a diner in New

York, in the winter of 1969, passing through town, reading the Vega of Dostoevsky's oeuvre, when I looked up and saw a bum staring at me through the window as if it were a mirror. He had a dirt-creased brown face, long beard, sunken black eyes. Sleet hit him as he stood there; then he staggered away in his long, gray overcoat rent in the tail, reminding me it wasn't just a novel.

A Wake in Ybor City
By José Yglesias

I read this novel when I was in my early twenties, a proletarian love song set in the Cuban community in Tampa, Florida, in 1958, the Tampa I knew from my childhood. I never owned a copy of the book, but used to take it out of the library once a year or so to hear the voices of the three Cubana sisters, Clemencia, Mina, and Dolores, sitting on the porch in Ybor City. One day I went to the library to check the book out and it was gone, put up for sale due to lack of use. The novel was long out of print, so I tracked down José Yglesias and wrote him a letter. The address I mailed it to was old, he'd moved, but the letter was forwarded and a month or two later I received a reply from Maine. He was flattered that I was such an aficionado of his first novel, and he agreed to send me a photocopy of the book; it was the best he could do, he explained, since he had only one or two copies left. We began corresponding, and I read more of his books. *The*

Truth about Them and *The Goodbye Land* I admired, but *A Wake in Ybor City* captured a special place in my heart. Finally, we arranged to meet, in New York City, where he now lived. My son Asa and I went first to Cooperstown, New York, to visit the Baseball Hall of Fame following his graduation from high school in California. I told Asa we would be meeting José and how attached I'd become to this particular novel over the years. The day before we left Cooperstown, we stopped into a used bookstore and just for fun I checked to see if they had any of Yglesias's books. They had one, a pristine copy of *A Wake in Ybor City*. This was a small miracle, of course, and I bought it for five dollars. I'd never seen a copy other than the one the library had discarded. José signed it for me the next afternoon in the restaurant where we met for lunch. We became friends, and I saw him every time I was in New York City until he died in 1995 at the age of seventy-five. The real miracle was that I liked José as much as I liked his beautiful first novel.

The Makioka Sisters
By Junichiro Tanizaki

Tanizaki was a very modern Japanese writer, a bohemian of the 1920s and after, who was drawn to the West but sensitively re-created the Tokyo of pre–World War II in this, his greatest novel. I read it in 1975, while I was in Japan for the first time; without it, I doubt that I could have really understood the underlying reasons that people there behaved as they did. Foremost was the sense of obligation and how excruciatingly difficult it was—and in some cases still is—to act with free will. When I first arrived in Kyoto, I was looking for a particular address and couldn't find it. I stopped in a small food shop and a young guy there offered to take me to it. He left his shop and walked me ten minutes to the place. Nobody was home but a passerby said he knew the person I was looking for and offered to take me to his house to wait. The shopkeeper went back to his place after I thanked him profusely, and I went with the passerby, whose name, he told me in English, was Sailor. We drank tea and sake together for a couple of hours. He was a poet and musician. I asked him how he had gotten the name of Sailor, and he told me he had taken it for himself because he was sailing along through life. Sailor looked to be in his early to mid-thirties. Eventually the person I was looking for returned, I thanked Sailor for his hospitality and left. I never saw him again, but thirteen years later, when I wrote *Wild at Heart*, I named my protagonist Sailor.

Snow Country
By Yasunari Kawabata

A completely different type of writer than Tanizaki, Kawabata was, compared to him, a kind of miniaturist.

The beautiful images Kawabata paints are contrasted with his surgical thrusts to the heart, lethal blows landed strategically and so swiftly that the reader is unable to avoid the avalanche that follows. Kawabata employed a method called *shosetsu*, defined by the eminent translator Edward Seidensticker as "a piece of autobiography or a set of memoirs, somewhat embroidered and colored but essentially nonfiction." Mr. Seidensticker has noted that, while *shosetsu* contains elements of fiction, it is "a rather more flexible and generous and catholic term than 'novel.'" Kawabata's books seem pure but underneath the serenity is often a terrible, unspeakable brutality.

Chinatown
By Robert Towne

Yes, of course, this is a screenplay, but it is the only screenplay I've ever read—except, perhaps, for Lem Dobbs's *Edward Ford*—that reads like a novel. The amazing thing is that it worked so brilliantly as a film. Preston Sturges's screenplays, especially *Hail, the Conquering Hero* and *The Miracle of Morgan's Creek*, read a little like novels but their fractured artifice shows, you know they're written to be movies. *Chinatown* isn't like them, it moves as characters are being developed and *you see as you read*. This is a remarkable accomplishment.

Masters of Atlantis
By Charles Portis

A comic masterpiece. Read also his novel *The Dog of the South*. Portis was chief of the London bureau of the *New York Herald-Tribune*, I believe. Made his money on his Western novel, *True Grit*, made into a John Wayne movie. Neither that novel nor the movie interested me, but *Atlantis* is a work of genius that probably not too many people have read. Portis is from Arkansas, and still lives there as of this writing. This book would crack up God, if He had a sense of humor.

The Stranger
By Albert Camus

Camus made the most compelling argument against capital punishment in a long essay wherein he eloquently opposed the use of the state as executioner. I've never been opposed to capital punishment per se; however, far too many people have been put to death mistakenly, a problem that is being somewhat rectified by the use of DNA testing; and then there is the economic factor, which is a de facto condition. Race prejudice, of course, plays a major role in this situation. The answer is to remove the impersonal element of the punishment. There really are cases in which guilt is proven beyond a doubt; if a capital offense has been committed against someone—a child, say, who has been brutally raped and murdered—I believe the parents of the victim should be given the opportunity to end the life of the person or persons responsible. If they choose not to do so, then life imprisonment without possibility of parole should be mandatory. God has nothing to do with it; killing is a temporal matter.

The Maigret Novels
By Georges Simenon

As a detective, Maigret is a disaster. It's a good thing these stories have nothing to do with truth. The perpetrator is identified early on in them, if not immediately. Inspector Maigret and his mild bunch at the Quai des Orfèvres are tipsy most of the time; at least they are clever enough to let the crimes solve themselves. The delightful part of the dozens of Maigret novels is the atmosphere and the comfort they provide; it's a world Simenon knows nothing about, he made it up, especially the police proceedings. The character of Maigret himself is a ruse. Even Simenon was a phony Frenchman; he was Belgian. He claimed to have had sexual relations with more than a thousand prostitutes and apparently abused his daughter, who eventually committed suicide. It's a cozy world in these books: the warm bars on the typically cold, rainy Paris afternoons (and mornings); the grey river divulging corpses; Mme. Maigret, plump and always ready to please, quick with a meal and a bottle for her man in their stuffy flat near Bastille. Simenon went to live for years in Arizona; he liked wide open spaces, dreamed of being a cowboy. A bad man who wrote hundreds of books, most of them good. His method, he said, was to check into a hotel room and emerge a week to ten days later with a finished novel. He wrote potboilers, used very few words. I learned a lot from Simenon's work; too bad he was such an ugly customer off the page.

Hunger
By Knut Hamsun

An early influence on me, this novel moved me because it examined man's cruelty to man in a way that felt real, as Nelson Algren did a generation later. Hamsun was a Nazi sympathizer, maybe worse, but there is still truth in this book that doesn't go away. I think of a man in a threadbare overcoat and rent shoes shuffling through the snow, leaving a trail of gray blood beneath a bland, sunless sky.

Homo Faber
By Max Frisch

The original *Fear of Flying*. Alternate title: *Death and the Daughter*. Bruno Bettelheim wrote a great essay on Freud and man's soul, about how Freud's writings had been mistranslated into English and his ideas, therefore, misunderstood. We are all misunderstood, aren't we? What a pleasure to be able to blame it on a bad translation. Man makes his own bed and sometimes he lies down in it with the wrong person, which can't always be helped. The problem is that sometimes he can't get back up.

The Short Stories of Irwin Shaw

Forget the later, grossly commercialized work such as *Rich Man, Poor Man*; you can even ignore the early hit *The Young Lions*. The great contribution to literature made by Shaw resides in his short stories, many—*many*—of which are superb, not just good. Herb Gold once said to me that Irwin should always be remembered just for the title of his story, "Girls in Their Summer Dresses." "The Eighty-Yard Run," "A Year to Learn the Language," and "In the French Style" are among my favorites, but there are at least a dozen more that should be read and reread. The director Robert Parrish, who filmed Shaw's "In the French Style" (a conflation of the latter two above-mentioned stories), which Shaw coproduced from his own script, told me that Shaw wanted to be in the movie business so he could screw actresses. In this pursuit, Shaw has certainly not been alone. The film wasn't great, the demarcation between the two stories was too obvious, but I'll bet Irwin had some fun on and off the set. I met Shaw a year or two before he died when he was staying at the Sherry Netherland Hotel in New York. I visited him in his suite, where he was meeting with Dustin Hoffman, who was considering doing Shaw's play *Bury the Dead* in a Broadway revival. (Hoffman wound up doing Arthur Miller's *Death of a Salesman* instead.) We got to talking about William Saroyan, who had recently died, and Hoffman told a suspect story about a telephone conversation he'd had with Bill. After Hoffman left, Shaw told me he knew Hoffman wouldn't do *Bury the Dead*, despite the actor's professed enthusiasm for the project. "Actors are the most unreliable people on the planet," Shaw said. I didn't ask him what he thought about actresses.

Far from the City of Class and *A Mother's Kisses*
By Bruce J. Friedman

For a while in the 1960s, Bruce J. Friedman was almost always right on the money with his stories, especially the ones that were set in his native Bronx. The title story of the collection *Far from the City* centers on his experience while he was in exile from the Bronx attending the University of Missouri, in Columbia, which institution I also attended, briefly, in 1964–65. Friedman was far from home, from what was familiar to him, and he rendered the feeling perfectly, hysterically, nastily. He did it even better in his novel *A Mother's Kisses*, when the protagonist goes to the sticks (the college in the wilderness) with his zany, zaftig Jewish mother. It's the duck out of water nightmare matched with the immigrant–Marilyn Monroe–money and madness sad sack craziness of America. Friedman seemed to lose his way with his fiction after he went to Hollywood, and never really did get all the way back on track; but these two books are brilliant, ur-American classics. Whaddayamean whaddaImean?

Libra
By Don DeLillo

I have an aversion to novels that use historical figures, real people as characters, such as *Ragtime*. If you can make up a story, make up a name, for God's sake. I'm sorry, but Benjamin Franklin probably did not whistle "When the Moon Comes over the Mountain" while he was taking a whiz in the moonlight. *Based* on Ben Franklin called Sam Black, okay; only don't use the man's real name because you don't know that he actually did that thing. Got it? DeLillo's *Libra* is my one exception: his use of the legend of Lee Harvey Oswald is so ingenious, the novel is so well conceived, structured, and written, that I give him a pass. I believe every creepy piece of this. Oswald went to high school in New Orleans across the street from Mandina's restaurant, which has the best fried chicken in town.

I Should Have Stayed Home
By Horace McCoy

McCoy was not a great writer. He wrote *They Shoot Horses, Don't They?* which became his most famous book, and he wrote screenplays for B movies. This one captures the real Hollywood slice of lowlife in a minimalist way; *You Play the Black and the Red Comes Up* by Eric Knight is a phony pastiche job next to this. It's too bad that Sal's Martoni, my old favorite sleazy haunt on Cahuenga, is gone now. It was a great late-night spot to get a plate of pasta al pesto and a decent martini and/or a girl, drugs, whatever you really needed at two A.M. When my daughter, Phoebe, graduated from UCLA, she asked me to take her to Martoni's for dinner that night. Phoebe's not only my girl but my *kind* of girl.

My Friends
By Emmanuel Bove

I've got my gripes with the French and so did Bove, who was French. Actually, this little novel taught me not only what to leave out but what was never there in the first place. Think about a one-legged cricket still trying to rub its legs together. Bove, having once heard the sound, pretends to hear it again. I once saw a one-legged man dancing in a joint on the rue de Lappe, his partner turning and twirling expertly so that his one foot never left the floor. Do words make a sentence?

Go in Beauty
By William Eastlake

Eastlake's Western trilogy, comprising *Go in Beauty*, *The Bronc People*, and *Portrait of an Artist with 26 Horses*, has been brushed under the literary rug, overshadowed by Cormac McCarthy's *Border Trilogy*, which is a shame, because Eastlake's books are better, far more original, less academic, and devoid of the kind of melodrama that sinks McCarthy in the end. If anyone talks about Eastlake's work these days, it's probably about his novel *Castle Keep*, which was made into a semicoherent movie with Burt Lancaster and Peter Falk. Eastlake was from New Jersey and moved to New Mexico, where he became a rancher. The feeling these novels provide is similar to that found in David Miller's film *Lonely Are the Brave*, which was based on the novel *The Brave Cowboy* by Edward Abbey, whose nonfiction book, *Desert Solitaire*, was his masterpiece. It's the passing of something, a time, a moment, that won't come again. All that's left is the whiff of memory.

The Black Mass of Brother Springer
By Charles Willeford

Charlie told me this was his own favorite among his books. It was first published under the title *Honey Gal* by some fly-by-night sleazoid paperback company. I promised him I'd republish it under his intended title in the Black Lizard Books series I was then editing. Charlie died before he saw it, but it was the last title published in the series. This is a Gila monster of a novel, colorful and awful; its teeth marks will still be on your hand after you finish it. Willeford, who gained renown before his death for his Hoke Moseley detective novels (*Miami Blues*, etc.), said the only writer of what the French call *policiers* who knew less about police procedure than he did was Georges Simenon.

The Short Stories of Somerset Maugham

I prefer Maugham's short stories to his novels, although when I was a teenager I thought very highly of *The Razor's Edge*, which had to do with finding true enlightenment and inner peace. It was presented rather simplistically, but Maugham had a way of making all of his stories seem personal, as if he had observed all of the doings firsthand. "Footprints in the Jungle," "The Letter" (made into a great movie with Bette Davis, who was also wonderful in the film of Maugham's novel *Of Human*

Bondage—her infantile waitress slut slapping painful clubfooted medical student suitor Leslie Howard with her withering, maddening response to his entreaties, "Ay down't moind" disturbs me still), "Honolulu," and dozens of other stories are unforgettable. Maugham was a good storyteller, not really a great writer, though he had success in the theater, too. The anthology films *Trio* and *Quartet*, made of his stories, are well done, but the endings were mostly changed, making them hopeful or happy as opposed to the bitter, more realistic endings of his stories as written. He lived into his nineties, I believe he graduated from medical school, he was homosexual, he went to a million parties, and he was perhaps the best listener there ever was. Maugham was unafraid of being mean in his work, and maybe in his personal life, I don't really know. When I think of Maugham, I see him sitting in a rattan chair on a verandah at Raffles Hotel in Singapore sipping a gin and tonic under a slowly whirling ceiling fan in a white suit looking forward to an evening of good conversation, a savory dinner, and later some smooth-skinned boy to chase the blues. Verandah, by the way, or veranda, was originally a Bengali or Hindi word adopted by the British.

The Tale of Genji
By Lady Murasaki (Murasaki Shikibu)

Most probably the first novel ever written, during the Heian era in Japan, more than 1,000 years ago. Edward Seidensticker's is the preferred English-language translation, the two-volume set. Before Murasaki, there was Sei Shonagon, a court lady, who kept *The Pillow Book*, her diary, that could be considered the first novel, seeing as how her observations of events were greatly embroidered and digressive. These women beat Daniel Defoe to the punch by a long shot, at least six hundred years, and they wrote better and more compellingly. See also Ivan Morris's writings on the Heian era, specifically *The World of the Shining Prince*. In rural northern Japan in 1975, I traveled for a while with a big Mongolian-Japanese guy named Rinchu, who wore only traditional dress and carried a small sword in defiance of the law. He also went against convention by eating as we walked. Rinchu wore his hair long, tied back, like a samurai. Residents of villages in Hokkaido that we passed through always stared at us disapprovingly, a *gaijin* and a wandering rogue. Outside Asahigawa we encountered a little old man with a long white beard carrying a load of sticks on his back. The old man appeared suddenly in our path from the forest and spoke to us as he passed. I asked Rinchu what the old man said, and Rinchu told me, "The mountain is our mother."

The Cool World

By Warren Miller

I'll never forget the fourteen-year-old girl who'd never been out of Harlem and didn't know what an ocean was. The other kids take her to Coney Island, I think, she disappears, and they never see her again. Shirley Clarke made a good little movie based on this novel, and once I talked on the phone to Warren Miller's widow, Jimmie, who wrote a book called *The Big Win*. My friend Richard Price said that *The Cool World* was a big influence on him, and he became more than a pretty good writer. About as far from the *World of the Shining Prince* as you can get, but I like to think of the girl who got lost at the beach as the Harlem Princess of the Waves.

The Talented Mr. Ripley

By Patricia Highsmith

Highsmith's parents were doctors (one of them anyway), and when she was eight years old she began reading Karl Menninger's *The Human Mind*, his casebook on human personality. Highsmith said that every emotion, motive, and form of madness was documented by the Kansas doctor, and from this compendium she drew the characters and plots for her stories and novels. Her first novel, *Strangers on a Train*, was famously filmed by Alfred Hitchcock, and in this case the movie is definitely superior to the book. Hitchcock made changes that actually accelerated the tension while simplifying the action; it was also wonderfully conceived, especially the nail-biter toward the end where a gnome-like carny crawls under an out-of-control ride to save the day. That wasn't in the novel. The book was clumsily written, the prose unremarkable, but the suspense was intact. Highsmith's work was decidedly uneven; only her Ripley novels were first-rate, and not all of them. *The Talented Mr. Ripley* is by far the best. I was impressed by it because of her creation of a murderer who is also likeable; at least, ingenuous. It's been filmed twice, to no really good effect (René Clément's version, *Purple Noon*, is much better than Anthony Minghella's slick, tedious attempt). The best film version of her work so far is Wim Wenders's *The American Friend*, which conflates two other Ripley novels, *Ripley Underground* and *Ripley's Game*. Highsmith was a lesbian, an alcoholic, who, apparently became increasingly racist and anti-Semitic as she grew older. She was born in Fort Worth, Texas, and was very pretty during her youthful adulthood, which she spent mostly in New York City during the 1950s and '60s. Then she moved to Europe, living the majority of the time in Switzerland. She went back to the Ripley well later with *The Boy Who Followed Ripley*, which employed an overtly gay theme, but the novel wasn't any good. It was Highsmith who turned me on to *The Human Mind*, which became almost as indispensable a sourcebook for me as the Bible. Nobody in her books is ever really happy, and I'm sure she wasn't, either.

The Subterraneans
By Jack Kerouac

Do yourself a favor and listen to Kerouac read the excerpt from this short novel that he recorded in 1958, or thereabouts. He achieves his goal of creating jazz prose—you can tap your foot to it. In March 1965, I was sitting in a café in Columbia, Missouri, the Agora House, reading *The Subterraneans*, when the assistant baseball coach from the University of Missouri, which I was ostensibly attending, spotted me through the front window. He came in and asked why I hadn't been at baseball practice that day. I admitted that I'd been reading and lost track of the time. He told me I was betraying the team and myself and stalked off to report my delinquency to the head coach. I knew then that my baseball life was about at an end. I had another idea, and that spelled trouble, if not certain death, for an athletic career. By the end of May that year, I was living in Europe, writing poetry, and I never went back to school. I was a pretty good third baseman then, just as Kerouac had been a pretty good freshman halfback at Columbia University; but when it comes to sports, pretty good isn't good enough. The writing of literature is in another ballpark altogether.

Lion at My Heart
By Harry Mark Petrakis

I don't think it's much of a stretch to say that Petrakis is a generally forgotten writer these days (2003); especially if one considers even William Saroyan more rather than less passé. Petrakis was a Chicagoan, son of a steel-mill worker; he may even have worked in the mills himself for a time. The family were Greek immigrants, tough, new Americans in the first part of the twentieth century. Petrakis gained some notoriety for his novel *A Dream of Kings*, mostly because it bore resemblance to Kazantzakis's *Zorba the Greek*. I met Eleni Kazantzakis in Paris in about 1982, and we corresponded for a few years after that (after Nikos's death, she lived in Switzerland). I asked her if she had read Petrakis, and she said she had not. I told her his ethnic, coming-of-age first novel, *Lion at My Heart*, was very touching and that it reminded me a little of Nelson Algren's work. Eleni Kazantzakis, who impressed me, an unpretentious, elegant lady, filled with sincere concern for the downtrodden of the earth, responded, "Algren creates so many uncouth characters, doesn't he?" I replied that Algren didn't have to go very far in order to create them because their models were people Algren saw every day in Chicago. I read an interview once with Petrakis, and it disappointed me in that he sounded a bit pompous and insulted that he wasn't famous. *Lion at My Heart* has some touching scenes in it between father and (not very) rebellious son, similar to those in Kerouac's *The Town and the City*; but I think of it favorably in the same vein as Jose Yglesias's *A Wake in Ybor City* and Saroyan's Fresno stories. Petrakis, Saroyan, and Yglesias are forgotten, really; they're rarely read and/or discussed, but I'll remember them for as long as I live. And while you're at it, watch Joseph Mankiewicz's film *House of Strangers* (1949); the scenes between Edward G. Robinson and Richard Conte are what I'm talking about.

Manhattan Transfer and *The USA Trilogy*
By John Dos Passos

I read *USA* straight through in one week when I was a teenager in Tampa, Florida, and I read its predecessor, *Manhattan Transfer*, right after that. Even though *Transfer* doesn't employ the same newsreel technique as *USA*, I think they belong together: four novels that make a pretty good job of explaining what went on in America in the first half of the twentieth century. Dos Passos was a kind of radical thinker early on; he wrote an impassioned plea on behalf of Sacco and Vanzetti; lost an eye somewhere; was a pal, then an enemy of Hemingway's (in this, he certainly wasn't alone); and became a kind of conservative toward the end of his life. Oh yeah, now I remember: Dos Passos was in a car wreck in which his wife was killed—that's how he lost an eye. Hemingway liked Dos Passos's wife, so he blamed Dos for her death and did his best to revile him privately and publicly thereafter. Kerouac stole the end for *The Town and the City* from the end of *The Big Money* ("Vag"), the last of the *USA* novels. My father was an immigrant, and I thought about how tough he and his father and mother and brother had to be to survive in the slums of New York and Chicago in the 1920s. It's all there in *Manhattan Transfer*. When I was about eight years old one day I was with my dad on Chicago Avenue, and I saw a bum pick up a filthy half of a doughnut from the sidewalk and sit down on the curb and eat it. My dad took a bill off his roll and stuffed it in the man's jacket pocket. The bum didn't stop eating.

We Think the World of You
By J. R. Ackerley

Not to be confused in the least with Harlan Ellison's story "A Boy and His Dog," this little novel could be titled "A Most Unusual Man and His Dog Beyond Dog." Actually, the dog is Johnny's, the incarcerated object of the protagonist's affection, called, I believe, Queenie. In Ackerley's nonfiction book about Tulip, the dog's real name, we are spared the human drama, but much of the canine action is the same. My longtime and now deceased friend Butch Hall had a dog named Beano, a female, whose nickname was Joan, because she was the Joan Crawford of dogs. Butch and Joan were inseparable, and had a relationship and communication both as unusual and intimate as that of Ackerley and Tulip/

Queenie. No, they did not have sex, but they were attuned to each other's moods in a way I had never before and have not since witnessed. That Beano/Joan passed away before Butch did was fortunate, because I really don't think she could have tolerated another keeper/companion. I know there is a group that thinks pets should not be considered "owned" by human beings, but in the case of Joan and Butch, I would say it was Butch who was "owned" by her. She couldn't baste a ham or light a cigarette, but she knew how to handle Butch, who was an intelligent drunk with a big heart and some terrible habits. He never really outlived her, either.

Hard Rain Falling
By Don Carpenter

This is a tough Portland, Oregon, street novel that deals with jail time and homosexuality that I've been after Gus Van Sant to make a movie of for years. I knew Don Carpenter for the last ten years of his life, which lasted only into his fifties. He had diabetes and other ailments and finally it all became too much for him and he shot himself. Don wrote the film *Payday*, in which Rip Torn plays a Hank Williams type who destroys himself early; it's a movie I love, and doesn't get the credit it deserves. In his last three or four years, Don and I would meet for lunch about once a month, when I was in town. He gave me a script he'd written based on the Bettie Page story. He said, "It's probably not very good, but it's the best I can do now." He was right, of course. Don wrote a number of novels and short stories, but *Hard Rain Falling* is a for real piece of work. He asked what hotel I stayed in when I was in Hollywood, and I told him the Sunset Marquis. Don said there are two kinds of writers, those who stay at the Sunset Marquis and those who stay at the Chateau Marmont. Don preferred the Chateau because he had crazy dreams there, often nightmares from which he would wake shouting. At the Sunset, he told me, he slept soundly, which was no good for a writer like him. The time he was describing was back in the 1970s and '80s, and the hotels—especially the Sunset—have changed considerably since those days. I knew what Don meant, of course: he liked to stir the shit and he liked to have his shit stirred, too. We had a mutual acquaintance whom he abhorred, a former publisher of his. Don expressed a desire to shoot this person's toes off with a Ruger Redhawk revolver. Diabetes had taken a couple or more of Don's own toes. "A sonofabitch like him deserves to suffer," Don said of his erstwhile publisher, "but it's all right if he doesn't, because suffering would probably make him a better human being and that I could not abide."

The Novellas of Martha Gellhorn

Hemingway's third and only pretty wife. She was a better writer than he was. I'm certain he knew this and couldn't take it. Even his sons liked her. She found the Finca Vigia in Cuba and wound up living out her long life in London. Gellhorn was also a fearless, brilliant war correspondent. I went to a party once in Cadogan Square in the 1980s, and I mentioned that Martha Gellhorn lived there but nobody knew who she was.

A Room with a View
By E. M. Forster

Books do furnish a room, as Anthony Powell so adroitly put it, and this is one. Tidy and right. I prefer it as a finished product to Forster's plea for connection in *Howards End*, and I never really did care so much what really happened in the Malabar caves (*A Passage to India*)—remember that the victorious nag in Lawrence's story "The Rockinghorse Winner" is named Malabar. *Maurice*, Forster's posthumously published "gay" novel, is very good, and touching, too. In *Interesting Times*, the autobiography of former commie Cambridge historian Eric Hobsbawm, he writes of befriending Forster toward the end of Forster's life and ferrying him one evening in the early 1960s from Cambridge (where Forster lived in digs at Trinity—I once saw him there, walking across a lawn, wearing a cape; he resembled a large anteater) to London to attend a performance given by Lenny Bruce. Talk about worlds colliding! Hobsbawn reports that the encounter resulted in something less than a connection.

Don Quixote
By Miguel de Cervantes

Never underestimate the importance of sidekicks. As a kid, I was always aware of how the so-called hero really could not function as such without his *compañero*, especially in cowboy movies. Guys like Fuzzy Knight, Pat Buttram, Gabby Hayes, Leo Carillo were my Sancho Panzas in the Old West, courtesy of Republic, Monogram, and RKO. The Nashville Network used to rerun old cowboy pictures in a series hosted by Gene Autry and Pat Buttram. These codgers could barely move a muscle, let alone hop up on a cayuse, but they were a riot sometimes to listen to. They were showing a Sunset Carson or Johnny Mack Brown movie—no, it was a Hoot Gibson—and at the breaks they would make comments such as, "Ol' Hoot was quite a buckaroo, wasn't he, Pat?" "Yeah, Gene. Recall that time he shot up them fellers outnumbered him forty to one had him cornered in a canyon?" "They don't make 'em like that anymore, Pat." I wondered if Gene was referring to Hoot or the absurd Westerns that played such a big part in forming my and my childhood friends' characters. "Hey, Roy, you're bleedin' mighty bad. We got to get you to a doc." "It ain't nothin', Lucky, just a flesh wound." These guys got shot in the arm so many times it's a wonder one of 'em didn't just fall off. (In Raoul Walsh's Western *Pursued*, the wing-shot Dean Jagger's arm *does* fall off!) Gabby Hayes was probably my favorite of these sidekicks. He had his own TV program that came on about four o'clock in the afternoons. Gabby had a big, grizzled beard and always appeared to be chawin' tabacky. The show was sponsored by Puffed Wheat and Puffed Rice, which cereals he would shoot out of a cannon. Just before lighting the fuse, he'd shout, "Shot from guns!" They just don't make 'em like that anymore, either.

The Last of the Vikings
By Johan Bojer

A lost tale of the fishermen in the Danish Lofoten Islands, a hard and hardy bunch battling the icy seas, a combination of Jack London's Yukonians and the Sicilian *pescatores* dramatized by Luchino Visconti in *La Terra Trema*. Didn't these guys ever want to take off for Tahiti? This is the question I always asked myself when reading about men and women leading such miserable, difficult lives, freezing to death without a break. Maybe they didn't know that Tahiti existed, or even the Costa del Sol. In Bergman's movies everybody wants to commit suicide, and they don't want to bring children into such a dark, depressing world. When my mother left me once in Chicago during the winter when I was little, I was convinced it was hell and that I'd been lied to: hell was cold, not hot. I still feel that way.

The Opposing Shore
By Julien Gracq

My friend Georges Luneau first told me about Gracq in Paris in the early 1980s. Georges is a director, and wanted to make a film of *Le Rivage des Syrtes*, the French title, but Gracq wouldn't let him. The writer told Georges that this was his favorite book, and he didn't want to risk being misinterpreted. Georges made a movie of Gracq's *La Presqu'île*, instead, with the *nouvelle vague* actor Gérard Blain and one of Tony Curtis's ex-wives, a German woman whose name I don't remember. It's a beautiful picture, very simple; the story is nothing like that of *The Opposing Shore*, which is much more complex and takes place in either an ancient or future world. I could see why Gracq wanted to be careful about it. Gracq did win the Prix Goncourt for another novel, and he kept to himself in his flat in Paris, staying out of the public eye. He remained loyal to his tiny publisher, José Corti, whose office I used to walk past often on the rue de Vaugirard when I lived in the neighborhood, and worked most of his life as a teacher. Gracq created a world of serene mystery wherein beauty and treachery seemed inextricably wedded. This is my favorite description in the novel: "Piero Aldobrandi, unhelmeted, was wearing the black cuirass and the red commander's scarf and carrying the baton which linked him forever to this scene of carnage. But the figure, turning its back to the spectacle, relegated it to the mere status of landscape, and the face, strained by a secret vision, was the emblem of a supernatural detachment." The actress in Luneau's movie was Christine Kaufmann.

Macbeth
By William Shakespeare

Sure, it's fiction, isn't it? This is my favorite among Shakespeare's plays, and it reads like a novel, the way Robert Towne's screenplay for *Chinatown* does. The character of the deranged, diabolical Lady Macbeth makes her a shoo-in as the model for all manipulative, controlling, insecure wives on this planet or any other. Of the film versions, I like Welles's (he also did an all African American stage version of the play in New York at the same time he was doing "The Shadow" on the radio), and I like Polanski's; but the one I prefer is Akira Kurosawa's *Throne of Blood*, starring Toshiro Mifune as the outrageously henpecked king of the samurai. Toru Takemitsu, the composer, with whom I collaborated on a libretto for his opera, *Madrugada*, wrote ninety film scores, many for Kurosawa, including *Dodes'ka-den*, *Ran*, and *Kagemusha*. He told me a bizarre story about Kurosawa. One night he and the director were very drunk, and Kurosawa suggested they pay a visit to Mifune, from whom Kurosawa had been estranged for several years, ever since his once main actor had defected to Hollywood. Kurosawa ordered his limo driver to take them to Mifune's house, which was in the Beverly Hills of Tokyo, a quiet neighborhood, at three o'clock in the morning. Kurosawa and Takemitsu got out of the car and stood on Mifune's lawn. The director was a big man, over six feet tall, unusual for a Japanese; and Toru-*san* was tiny, frail, a complete contrast to Kurosawa. So there they were, the Japanese Mutt and Jeff, passing a bottle of whiskey back and forth, as Kurosawa shouted insults at Mifune's house. "You bastard son of a bitch! Washed-up has-been!" Takemitsu told me Kurosawa couldn't have known if the object of his invective was at home. (I remembered that Mifune had starred in a movie of Kurosawa's called *The Bad Sleep Well*.) Toru-*san* said he didn't see any signs of life inside the house. Finally, Kurosawa said, "Let's piss on his grass!" The director took out his cock and proceeded to urinate on Mifune's lawn. (I forget whether Takemitsu followed suit.) After he was finished, Kurosawa shouted a few more epithets, then he and Takemitsu got back into the limo and were driven away. Toru-*san* told me that a couple of days later he related this episode to a mutual friend of his and Kurosawa's and asked him not to repeat it. "What do you mean?" replied the friend. "Akira-*san* does this all the time! Mifune doesn't even bother to wake up anymore and chase him away."

Finnegans Wake
By James Joyce

A dream that never ends. Listening to Joyce read from it is a special treat. The British Library has a recording of him reading a long passage, perhaps eight or ten minutes, and his voice is so sprightly, mellifluous, precise, natural, it flows like the Liffey. The book came more alive for me when I heard Joyce's voice, so light, nimble, and ready. It's music, a love song to his own time and place, a city that never moved no matter where he lived or died.

Serenade
By James M. Cain

Cain is justifiably famous for his novels *The Postman Always Rings Twice*, *Double Indemnity*, and *Mildred Pierce*; mostly, I daresay, due to the fact that terrific films were made during the 1940s based on them. *Mildred Pierce* is less well written than the others but the title character and story have become unforgettable because of Joan Crawford's career-defining portrayal of a lower-middle-class divorcee striving to succeed so that her daughter can have the good things in life, only to discover that sisterhood ain't necessarily all that powerful no matter how carefully the cake is baked or the pie sliced (those familiar with the story will dig that crack). But it's *Serenade* that's Cain's true masterpiece, a cockeyed kind of epic about an opera singer (which Cain's mother intended he be) who loses his voice, finds himself penniless as well as voiceless, a sad sack competing for handouts with the starving masses on the mean streets of Mexico City (the masses are still there). The wingless warbler takes up with a Tepito prostitute who restores his manhood (more on that point later) and, more miraculously, his voice. The pièce de résistance comes fairly early in the story, involving sacrilegious sex, a thunderstorm, buckets of blood, and an iguana. After this, the preposterous accelerates rather than attenuates. The big warbler becomes a Hollywood movie star, makes a heroic comeback at the Metropolitan Opera in New York, a radio mogul (no TV yet), all in the depths of the Great Depression (mid-1930s), and drags along the Mexican Indian whore he's smuggled across the border and attempted to restyle as a classy *Norteamericana*. This last part falls apart fast—you can take the *chica* off the street but you can't take the street out of the *chica*, it says here—and then the real horror rises up in the form of the warbler's pansy past. The Mex chick turns *torera*, a malevolent gay guy gets his, there's a torrid denouement down Mexico way despite the best efforts of an opera buff Irish ship's captain (a character soon stolen by Orson Welles for his *Lady from Shanghai*), and the half-fairy (Cain's coin) winds up twisting and twisted in Tepito. *Serenade* is a semi-hysterical masterpiece and it's a tragedy that the film made from it was a not-bloody-at-all mess starring the oafish Mario Lanza (Elvis's idol), a monstrosity of a soaper directed by the usually reliable

Anthony Mann, the only saving grace being the appearance of the beauteous Sarita Montiel (who almost stole *Vera Cruz* from Saints Lancaster and Cooper). And, for a very good reason, it's the iguana who gets the last laugh.

Journey to the End of the Night
By Louis-Ferdinand Céline

The anti-Semitic mad doctor of France, their last great writer. It's significant that French literature ended here, at the pen of a marvelously inventive loony. Kerouac liked to remark that the book closed with Céline micturating into the Seine; it doesn't, but I know what he meant. The truth is that Céline pissed on everybody, including himself. He's the paranoid dreamer, creeping in a black cape through the sewers of the locus ceruleus. Take a shot from this man and you'll never be the same.

The Bible (Old and New Testament, King James Version)

The mother of all novels, a product of many hands. I've used it as a reference book during the writing of most of my novels. What would Cormac McCarthy, William Faulkner, or even Bob Dylan have done without it? Bloody, belligerent, contradictory, inchoate, crackpot, perfect, beautiful, bizarre, cause of a billion deaths and lives gone wrong. The Old Testament is the original noir novel, Eve the original femme fatale and Mary Magdalene the neighborhood bad girl. (By comparison, the New Testament is science fiction.) "The snorting of his horses was heard from Dan: the whole land trembled at the sound of the neighing of his strong ones; for they are come, and have devoured the land, and all that is in it; the city, and those that dwell therein. For, behold, I will send serpents, cockatrices, among you, which will not be charmed, and they shall bite you, saith the Lord."—Jeremiah 8:16/17. It serves every purpose under heaven, as was intended. The Bible is the windshield and the rest of us scribblers merely bugs upon it. When the rain comes, we get wiped away.

FILM AND TELEVISION

The Cavalry Charges

In 1995, when Francis Coppola asked me to adapt Jack Kerouac's novel *On the Road*, to which he owned the dramatic rights, into a screenplay, I was extremely flattered. His associate, Tom Luddy, came to see me, proclaiming that my novel *Wild at Heart* was "the *On the Road* for the 1990s," and that he and Francis wanted me to take a crack at helping turn Kerouac's modern classic, which many deemed unfilmable, into a feature film.

Neither Francis nor Tom knew of my previous experience with Kerouac's work, specifically the 1978 oral biography *Jack's Book* that I had coauthored with Lawrence Lee, which was still in print. I had first read *On the Road* when I was twelve years old and had read and reread Kerouac's books ever since. This information bolstered Francis's decision to hire me, and we began our discussions as to how to approach the material.

Francis believed the novel to be short on story and laden with more than one too many cross-country (and Mexican) trips. He asked me if I believed I could create a story. I told him that the story was already there: a search for the lost father of Dean Moriarty, the main character;

On the Road was about fathers and sons. Also, Kerouac had crafted a detailed, poetic portrait of America in the years immediately following World War II (the period covered in the novel is 1948–49), a chronicle of the changing face of the country after its most traumatic event since the Civil War. This perceptive sociological portrait, I explained, served as a panoramic backdrop for the intense, often frenetic search for not only the missing father but for the identities of the novel's two wandering protagonists. I would synthesize the multiple trips into one and a half, I said, without, I believed, having to sacrifice any of the most important and interesting action.

Before embarking on the screenplay itself, I offered to write an extended treatment that would include sample scenes, to make clear my intentions and to make certain that Francis and I were on the same page. At this point in the project, Coppola's intention was to direct as well as produce the movie, and he accepted my offer.

Francis approved the treatment, and I wrote the first draft of the screenplay. After he'd read it, Coppola called and congratulated me on doing exactly as I'd said I would, and said that he now not only understood the story but saw how it could be filmed in a linear fashion. At one time, he admitted, he and Luddy had considered doing a version of *On the Road* wherein the protagonists, Dean Moriarty and Sal Paradise, drove across a present-day Soviet Union, not the post–World War II United States. This invention, I averred, was one I doubted my ability to ever embrace.

Then I received a phone call from Fred Fuchs, at the time chief of production of Zoetrope Studios, Coppola's company. Fred told me that Francis had decided, following the success of his recent directorial effort, *Bram Stoker's Dracula*, to limit his participation in our project to a producer's role, leaving the direction to someone else. Fred and Francis's choice, Fred said, was Gus Van Sant, a choice with which I wholeheartedly concurred. I loved Gus's work, I told Fred, especially *Drugstore Cowboy*. My agreement pleased Fuchs and Coppola, and we set up a date for all of us to meet and discuss revisions before Gus and I began work on a second draft.

During the subsequent session, which was conducted at Francis's estate next to the Niebaum-Coppola vineyards, formerly the Inglenook vineyards, in Napa County in Northern California, attended by Fred Fuchs, Francis, Gus Van Sant, my assistant, Matt Johnson, and I, we were discussing how a particular scene could be shot, and I suggested using a helicopter. At this, Francis exploded: "Do you know how expensive that would be in New York City? The writer never thinks about expenses," he continued. (I kept in mind that Francis had begun his career as a screenwriter—he won an Academy Award for *Patton*—and still was.) "Do you know," he asked, "what the three most dangerous words in a screenplay are?" "No," I answered, "what are they?" "The cavalry charges!" Francis said. "Three little words to the writer," he went on, "but what do they mean to the production? Three days and three million dollars. More!

And horses!" We all laughed. Francis had made his point. The man who'd made *Apocalypse Now*, one of the greatest films of all time, and one which had famously gone over budget, certainly knew what he was talking about. I almost remarked that this was coming from the horse's mouth, but I restrained myself.

Later that day, while Francis was grilling hamburgers on the porch of his house, he told us that he was content for the moment, having earned his way out of bankruptcy with the stupendous success of the *Dracula* picture. "The treasure is in the cave," he said with a smile. We had been joined for lunch by his business manager, to whom Francis mentioned that the previous day he'd spotted someone walking on his hillside across the road. "That's not your hillside, Francis," said the business manager. "You don't own that piece of property, it's attached to the Inglenook château." "I don't own it?" Coppola responded, seeming genuinely surprised, if not miffed. "No," the manager replied, "but it is for sale." "How much do they want?" asked Coppola. "Nine million dollars." "Nine million dollars!" Francis exclaimed. "Yes," said his business manager, "but that includes the château." "That's too much," mumbled Coppola.

As we ate, we discussed the screenplay and other things. I observed Francis closely. He seemed troubled now, agitated, his mind no longer focused on the film project. Toward the end of our lunch break, Coppola asked his business manager again, "How much did you say they want for that property?" "Nine million, Francis," the manager repeated.

As it turned out, despite eventually having our *On the Road* project green-lighted by Columbia Pictures, it was not produced. Francis's relations with Columbia became more complicated at that moment and Van Sant's and my version of the movie became a casualty of the political fallout. At least that's how it was explained to me after the fact by Fred Fuchs, who seemed seriously disappointed at the outcome.

Gus and I were disappointed, too, of course. In fact, it's the single most frustrating and disappointing experience I've had in my occasional career in the movie business. That said, however, I thoroughly enjoyed working with Coppola and Van Sant, both of whose continuing friendship I value highly.

Approximately three weeks following that day at Coppola's, I was watching the news on television when a picture of Francis came on the screen and the newscaster said, "Film director Francis Coppola today announced his purchase of the former Inglenook château and surrounding acreage for a price reported to be slightly below nine million dollars." I laughed and said aloud, "The cavalry charges!"

A Brief Dossier on *One-Eyed Jacks*

1. An Unforgettable Film

One-Eyed Jacks (1961). Directed by Marlon Brando. Starring Marlon Brando, Karl Malden, Pina Pellicer, Timothy Carey, Katy Jurado, Ben Johnson, and Elisha Cook Jr. Screenplay by Guy Trosper and Calder Willingham.

Brando never looked better than he did in this picture; in fact, he made certain—he was the director, after all—that he was downright beautiful, if fat around the edges, a tendency difficult for him to disguise even then. The opening scene is a beauty: Marlon, as Rio, or the Kid, is sweet-talking a classy señorita at her house, cooing in her ear and slipping a ring onto the third finger of her left hand, telling her it's the ring his mother gave him just before she died. The dark-eyed beauty melts as he insinuates his body into hers—the Kid knows he's about to carve another notch on his gun. Then Karl Malden, called Dad Longworth, who's been taking care of some business of his own, shows up and shouts that the law is hot on their trail—this is Sonora, Mexico, in 1880—they've got to hightail it pronto! Rio wrenches the ring his "mother" gave him on her deathbed off the señorita's finger, says "Sorry, honey," and splits with his compadre Dad, leaving her, with perspiring thighs and quivering lips, in a literal lurch.

Dad and the Kid are bandits, of course, and they take off for the mountains with the gold booty they've appropriated from a Mexican bank. They ride hard for the sierras and finally hunker down on a ridge, doing their best to hold off the troops. One of their horses goes down, they're trapped, and Dad goes for help, taking the gold with him while Rio holds his position. He does the best he can, keeps looking over his shoulder for his trusted *compañero* to come back for him, but the authorities close in. Dad's to hell and gone with the loot, betraying the Kid, and Brando surrenders with the bitter knowledge that his so-called best friend has abandoned him.

The Kid breaks jail eventually and, accompanied by a Mexican cellmate, picks up Dad Longworth's stale trail, tracking him to a town on the central California coast near Big Sur. It's been five long years since Dad left Rio for dead on the mountain, and Longworth has built himself a new life—with the aid of the stolen gold. He's now a sheriff, married to a handsome Mexican woman played by Katy Jurado (sturdier-looking a decade since her svelte *la victima* in Buñuel's *El Bruto*), and stepfather to Katy's pretty, barely post-adolescent daughter, played by Pina Pellicer (who later committed suicide).

When Rio shows up with not only his Mex escapee pal but a trio of low company, including Ben Johnson playing the kind of badass he did in *Vera Cruz* and *Shane*, old Dad knows the Kid is itching to burn "Vengeance Is Mine" like a racehorse i.d. on the inside of Longworth's upper lip. Dad is nervous not only about his own safety but about that of his wife and daughter, and the town bank. The sheriff pretends he's glad to see Rio, amazed he's still alive, tells The Kid a cock-and-bull story about how he couldn't get back to the mountain, how the gold got away and all sorts of mealymouthed bushwah. Rio just takes it easy, slow to rile, seething beneath the surface at Dad's lies. Dad knows Rio knows he's lying, and warns him to behave; this is a nice little town we got here, a good place to raise a family. Yeah, drawls Rio, I might just want to do that. Longworth snickers, says this ain't your kind of situation, Kid. Best if you moved on.

The Kid doesn't move on. He sniffs out Dad's daughter, gets a start on that, then brawls with Timothy Carey, a snarling Neanderthal thug who attacks Rio in a bar. The Kid shoots him dead (in self-defense), and for this Dad nails Rio, hauls him to a hitching post, and in view of the citizens smashes the Kid's gun hand with the butt of a rifle, pulverizing Rio's trigger finger. Dad orders him out of town and Rio limps away with his confederates to bide his time on a beach *ranchito* while his hand heals.

Ben Johnson and his partner Harv (Sam Gilman) deride the Kid's attempts to shoot again once his gun hand is sound enough to rehabilitate, and they're impatient to bust the bank. They don't care much about Rio's revenge motive—until he got hurt they kept a cool distance from him, having heard about the Kid's gunfighting prowess; but now he's damaged goods and they've got big doubts that Rio will ever be of real use to them. Disrespect doesn't pay off for much in a world of killers, of course, and the Kid does come back. All of the mean business we've been waiting for is played out to no good end, and it's worth the wait. There's a particularly chilling moment when Rio's jail friend is turned on by the bad brothers, but the scene itself is so poetically and beautifully set, on the windswept, cypress-spotted sand dunes of the Monterey coast, that the grisly part almost doesn't matter. In fact, the California littoral is a major player in the movie, making even the few tedious parts bearable. It's a long'un: 141 minutes of Brando's fumbling and mumbling, but it works, and often majestically.

According to film editor Paul Seydor, one of the first full-length screenplays Sam Peckinpah ever wrote was an adaptation of *The Authentic Death of Hendry Jones*, a 1956 novel by Charles Neider that was based on the lives of Pat Garrett and Billy the Kid. Neider set his story not in New Mexico, where Pat and Billy had known each other, but in California, and fictionalized Billy Bonney and Pat Garrett as Hendry Jones and Dad Longworth. Garrett had written a book called *The Authentic Life of Billy the Kid* from which, also according to Seydor (who was a great friend and confrere of Peckinpah's), Neider borrowed, lifting dialogue and various incidents. Peckinpah was hired to direct the film version in 1957, wrote the screenplay, which went through numerous vicissitudes, then was fired off the project.

Following Peckinpah's departure—he would go on to direct an unhappy version of these events, *Pat Garrett and Billy the Kid*, in 1973—five or six other director/writers, including Stanley Kubrick (who found Brando to be a less-than-candid and/or trustworthy piece of work), came and went, until finally, in 1960, Brando—who owned the book rights—directed the picture, ultimately retitled *One-Eyed Jacks*. Brando's opus isn't Billy Bonney's story—Arthur Penn, in 1958, gave it a try with *The Left-Handed Gun*, Paul Newman re-creating his role from TV's *Philco Playhouse* (though James Dean was supposed to have starred in the movie), with a screenplay by Gore Vidal; it was Stan Dragoti, in 1972, who made the best Billy the Kid film by far, *Dirty Little Billy*, with Michael J. Pollard as a whiny, mud-splattered, mutt-faced, cowardly, back-shooting punk killer—but Brando did a splendid job, bringing together a story of almost-epic proportions, using the big screen to force surrender as real cinema demands. That Brando never again directed a movie may or may not have been a good thing, but with *One-Eyed Jacks* he accomplished what more celebrated directors could seldom do: he made an unforgettable film. After he saw Paramount's final cut, however, Brando said: "Any pretension I've sometimes had of being artistic is now just a long, chilly hope."

One-Eyed Jacks is not a masterpiece, like Peckinpah's *The Wild Bunch*, but I'll always remember Brando's Rio, the Kid, goading Malden's Dad Longworth—these two had had it out before in *A Streetcar Named Desire* (1951)— "How you doin', Dad?" the Kid asks, fake-friendly, when he arrives in Sheriff Longworth's town, suppressing his hatred of the father figure he once loved and trusted who'd thrown him to the wolves. It may as well have been the poet saying, "How do you like your blue-eyed boy now, mister death?"

2. Brando

Where to begin with Marlon Brando? Arguably, Brando was the first authentic American movie star who had also been a great success in the theater. I never saw him on stage, but his rep from *Truckline Cafe* and *A Streetcar Named Desire* precedes him to *The Men*, his first movie, in which he portrayed a paraplegic. In retrospect this seemed an odd choice to me for Brando to have made for his film debut. It was a solid, down-to-earth, unsensational role, and my respect for Brando initially stemmed from this performance. The only other person I remember being in the movie is Jack Webb, of *Dragnet* fame—who, by the way, was terrific in *The Last Time I Saw Archie* and Billy Wilder's *Sunset Boulevard*, an underrated actor. After *The Men* Marlon made the film of *Streetcar* and *The Wild One*, which tore it for the old folks and the squares but thrilled the kids, even though Lee Marvin, as Brando's rival motorcycle gang leader, stole the movie. By the time (1954) Brando did *On the Waterfront*, he was an indelible icon in the pantheon of American Culture Vulturehood. "I coulda been a contenduh. I coulda been *some*body," he complained to Rod Steiger as his brother, Charlie, in the backseat of an automobile *with a Venetian blind over the rear window!* "Instead of a bum, which is what I am." As the broken-down pug, Terry Malloy, who was forced by Charlie and his gangster cohorts to take a dive so that they could go for the price on Wilson, the lucky stiff beneficiary of the fix, Brando edged toward immortality. But then he played in a long string of losing games (though I thought *Bedtime Story*, an overlooked comedy with David Niven, was a tiny riot), not really insuring his status among the gods until *Last Tango in Paris* and *The Godfather*. I've had European actors tell me they think Brando is "too obvious" a performer—to hell with them and their opinions picked out of the ashes of burnt-out cultures. Marlon Brando made Americans, in their wretched void of seemingly purposeful ignorance and dreamy nostalgias for places and times that never existed, *feel* something outside of themselves. Sure, he got grotesquely fat and Truman Capote called him an idiot and his son murdered his daughter's lover and then she killed herself and he had several wives and who knows how many children and he probably became clinically crazy years and years ago, but the guy did a lot of work that people will remember for a long time if not for always, and anyway he's from

Libertyville, Illinois (though born in Omaha), where I used to go swimming with my mother when I was a kid, and I remember the farms there, which are now suburban Chicago housing developments. Brando undoubtedly remembers the farms that were there, too, he lived on one, and Orson Welles was from rural Illinois, also. Homeboys, all homeboys, filled with longing, looking to create other worlds, and Brando did it despite what those lousy European actors say dropping cigarette butts into their espresso cups.

3. Timothy Carey

Now here's a character, a real character let alone a character actor. I'll never, ever forget Timothy Carey as the rifleman who shoots and kills the racehorse in Kubrick's *The Killing*, or as the mob thug in Cassavetes's *The Killing of a Chinese Bookie*, and certainly not as the drunken lout in *One-Eyed Jacks*. With a lock of lank black hair always falling over one eye, Carey careened around menacingly in whatever context he appeared. His voice was deep but he sounded as if he were always gargling, words bubbling up, burping at his listeners. Carey was big and darkly depraved looking—out-of-control scary, which often made him seem worse than Lawrence Tierney's troubled personae. If little kids saw him lurching along the sidewalk headed their way, they'd abandon their toys and run. I saw him on a late-night TV talk show, wearing a too-small Hawaiian shirt, detailing for the horrified host his life's work: the study of flatulence. He was deranged, not dangerous, I guessed. Tom Luddy, who worked for Francis Coppola, once gave me, for a reason I no longer remember, Timothy Carey's address and telephone number, which I still have in my directory—he lived in El Monte, California—but I never got in touch with him other than telepathically, and a few years ago he died. In an essay I wrote about an absurd little 1955 movie called *Finger Man*, I described Carey as being unequaled at the Unbridled Snarl. He couldn't control his hands or his hair. He justified the French intellectual's image of the typical American male. And just what do I know about how French intellectuals think? you may well ask. And while you're at it, exactly what—or who—is a typical American male?

4. Katy Jurado, Pina Pellicer, and Other Mexican Actresses

When referred to in magazine and newspaper articles, Katy Jurado was most always called "the fiery Katy Jurado." She played Gary Cooper's mistress in *High Noon* and the wife of Spencer Tracy in *Broken Lance* and, of course, the wife of Karl Malden in *One-Eyed Jacks*. In real life she was married for a time to the actor Ernest Borgnine, who called her "a tiger," but she always was a Mexican citizen. Katy never went Hollywood, she lived in Cuernavaca. She worked for Luis Buñuel in 1952 in his heavy-handed slice of life *El Bruto*, when she had her looks. She never rivaled Dolores del Rio or Maria Félix or even Rita Moreno, Isela Vega, or Movita (one of Marlon's wives) in the Drop Dead department, but Katy Jurado was always a convincing actress, even as Elvis Presley's mother. (In *Stay Away, Joe*.) Dolores del Rio was in *Flaming Star*, making Elvis probably the only American actor from Tupelo, Mississippi, to play opposite two Mexican movie stars in the 1960s. Jurado brought an air of dignity and intelligence to her film roles. I always believed that her character was smarter than any other character in the movie. And for some reason it pleased me to read in her obituary that she had a daughter who lived in Chicago.

Pina Pellicer died by her own hand very young. She was a lover of Brando's, who wrote in his autobiography that during the filming of *One-Eyed Jacks* he "slept with a lot of pretty women and had a lot of laughs." Pina Pellicer looked pretty fragile, pretty and fragile, on screen. I can't imagine life to her was a lot of laughs. I don't know anything about her, really, but in the movie she seems frightened and shy, the opposite of Katy Jurado, who played her mother. The only Mexican movie star I know is Salma Hayek, who seems quite adept at handling herself and getting along with people. I acted in a scene with her in a film in Venice, Italy, and Salma blew through it like a tiny tornado. She knew exactly what to do and how to do it well. My guess is that Pina Pellicer never possessed that kind of confidence, the kind you need to keep going. One of Maria Félix's five husbands was the great Mexican songwriter Agustín Lara, who sat at home at the piano in Mexico City and composed sad, heartbreaking laments ("Noche de Ronda," "Veracruz," "Solamente una vez," "Maria Bonita"—about Maria Félix) while his actress wife flamboyantly philandered around the world. And Orson Welles, having left his wife, Rita Hayworth, for Dolores del Rio, pronounced Pains of the River the most beautiful woman in the world, but he didn't marry her.

5. Karl Malden

The best nose in the business. Malden's proboscis looked like it had been fought over and chewed on and pitted and pulled and pried and done got elongated by a pride of lions wrestling over the last morsel on the plains of the Serengeti. Malden *intruded* into scenes several seconds after his nose entered the frame. Okay, enough about his schnozz. He was a heavy actor, a large gesture in a roomful of nuances. Stuck close to Brando: *Streetcar*, *Waterfront*, *Jacks*. I liked him in *The Cincinnati Kid*, another film almost directed by Sam Peckinpah (who got fired at the start). In *Cincinnati* he's got a sexy young wife, played by Ann-Margret, who cheats on him with Steve McQueen. (Can't imagine why.) Malden was always second fiddle but a block of granite nonetheless. I could imagine him playing on the offensive line at Rutgers with Vince Lombardi. When Stanley Kubrick said to Marlon Brando that he'd read the script for *One-Eyed Jacks* but couldn't understand what the movie was about, Brando told him: "This picture is about my having to pay two hundred and fifty thousand dollars a week to Karl Malden." Brando had signed Malden up, and each week the filming was delayed meant another $250,000 lost. Kubrick responded, "Well, if that's what it's about, I think I'm doing the wrong picture." So Kubrick didn't direct, and Sidney Lumet and Elia Kazan turned it down, too. Peckinpah never got an offer, and was even aced out of the screenplay credit. Apparently Brando dumped Peckinpah for Kubrick (who was only twenty-nine), and when Kubrick bailed, Brando had indeed to justify the commitment to Karl Malden or head for Teti'aroa (which he did later). Malden did a wonderful job as Dad Longworth—he knew just how to *appraise* Rio, how not only to look but to look *at*. As Rio's surrogate father he knew exactly how to make him squirm, despite his having ditched and left the Kid for good as dead back in the day. Malden knew how to put the mean into meaning and the meaning into mean, something a handsome man couldn't do.

6. Ben Johnson

A real cowboy, Ben Johnson was brought west from Texas by Howard Hughes in the 1940s to take care of his horses. He wound up in the movies and just about became a movie star. Hughes bought RKO so that he could date actresses, which he did by the boatload, and he even married a few. I don't have any idea what Ben Johnson's love life was like, but he maintained his sly-eyed good looks while working for John Ford, George Stevens, Brando, and dozens of others, capping his career with not only an Academy Award–winning performance for Peter Bogdanovich in *The Last Picture Show*, but slightly earlier for the man Marlon jilted, Sam Peckinpah, in *The Getaway* in 1972. In that film, based on a Jim Thompson novel, Johnson had the face and demeanor of a cruel wolf, torturer of Steve McQueen and Ali MacGraw, forcing them to grovel until they turn on him. By this time Ben Johnson knew just how to act, to keep a tension, to keep a hate on. But Johnson was at his very best in Peckinpah's *The Wild Bunch* (1969), for my money the best American movie ever made. He and Warren Oates play the Gorch brothers, Lyle and Tector—violent, whoring, hard-drinking, murderous, mother-grabbing sons of bitches—but *loyal* mother-grabbing sons of bitches, loyal to their ethos, their notion by God or the devil of what Right just might could be. When Ben and Warren join William Holden and Ernest Borgnine in their Mexican Death March from the whorehouse to General Mapache's hangout, hell-bound and *certain* because this is the end of the only way of life they know is worth living, they have no choice, and I look each time into Ben Johnson's eyes and he's got me fooled because I know he ain't acting in that moment, he's right there square in the narrow corner not called No Turning Back for nothing. Brando used Johnson to good advantage in *Jacks*, keeping him on the back burner while Brando did his star turn. Johnson goaded Brando good, he kept in character—but then Peckinpah and Bogdanovich took the halter off of Hughes's daddy's cowhand. Ben Johnson put his own brand on the movies. You can't miss it.

7. Slim Pickens and Elisha Cook Jr.

The most famous ride Slim Pickens ever took was on the nuclear bomb at the end of Kubrick's film *Dr. Strangelove*. Like Ben Johnson, Pickens was a cowhand and rodeo performer brought to Hollywood to lend Western movies a degree of authenticity. In *One-Eyed Jacks* he distinguished himself by portraying a craven deputy whom Rio bluffs with an unloaded Derringer into unlocking his cell door. Pickens transforms himself from a leering, wise-cracking, bullying liar into a crawling coward in a flick of an eyelash, his weak receded double chin quivering, Adam's apple palpitating as Brando humiliates him and locks Pickens up in his own jail. A regular in Western movies for decades, Slim Pickens became an accomplished comic actor—note his performance in *Rancho Deluxe*, as well as in the aforementioned *Dr. Strangelove*. Terry Southern, Kubrick's screenwriter on *Strangelove*, told this bizarre story about Pickens: when Slim met the African American actor James Earl Jones on the set,

Southern mentioned to Jones that Pickens had just finished filming *One-Eyed Jacks* with Brando. Jones politely inquired as to how it was working with the great Mr. Brando, and country boy Slim told him, "Wal, you know ah worked with Bud Brando for right near a full year, an' durin' that time ah never seen him do one thing that wudn't *all man* an' *all white*." Pickens had beady eyes, was always in need of a shave, didn't disguise his pot belly, and always made the movie he was in better. Toward the very end of *The Getaway*, he has a brief, wonderful scene with Steve McQueen when he sells his pickup truck to bank robber Doc McCoy and his wife, Carol (Ali MacGraw), both of whom he's stopped for on the road. Pickens's character drives a hard bargain but gladly takes an excessive offer from Carol, and just gets out on the highway, yells, "Yahoo!" and ambles bowleggedly away with his bonanza, a grin on his scraggly face the size of Texas, his birthplace.

Elisha Cook Jr. and Wallace Ford supposedly appeared in more films than any other actors in the history of the movies. Cook made a mark in *The Maltese Falcon*, *Shane*, *Born to Kill*, and dozens more. But it's really in Kubrick's masterpiece *The Killing* that Cook cooks the hottest. A pari-mutuel clerk at the racetrack his gang plans to rob, Cook is married to bombshell Marie Windsor, a devil dame who taunts her husband for not being a good enough provider along with his more obvious shortcomings, such as being short, ugly, wimpy, etc. Why did she marry him in the first place? She's a cheap whore who's got a man or more on the side. Cook brags to her about the big heist he and his cohorts are about to pull off, desperate to impress and keep her. She then blabs to a boyfriend about the scam, which causes the thing to blow up. Cook stumbles back to their seedy apartment after the disastrous denouement and murders her. This is his best performance, though Cook was always good, always tortured and pathetic, as weaselly gunsel Wilmer in *Falcon* or a hophead hotel bellboy being chewed to death by anxiety over what he'll never have or be. Elisha Cook Jr. conveyed what it means to be a Terrified Little Man better than anyone. He lived to be almost a hundred years old.

8. Sam Peckinpah and Stanley Kubrick

Sam Peckinpah had been fascinated by the story of Billy the Kid and Pat Garrett for years and wanted to do a movie about them. In 1956, he decided to write a screenplay based on Charles Neider's novel *The Authentic Death of Hendry Jones*, which he did, finishing it on November 11, 1957. Brando's Pennebaker Productions bought the book rights and Peckinpah was thrilled at the idea of scripting the picture. On May 12, 1958, Brando's company signed a contract with Stanley Kubrick for him to direct the movie for Paramount Pictures. Peckinpah revised his screenplay and handed it in on May 6, 1959. Kubrick didn't like it, and Brando dumped Peckinpah, who was understandably depressed by this decision. Kubrick hired Calder Willingham to rewrite the screenplay with him, but they apparently stalled on page fifty-two and hit a dead end. The film was by now retitled *One-Eyed Jacks*. Willingham, who (with Jim Thompson) had written *Paths of Glory* for Kubrick, was let go, as was Kubrick, who went to work on *Lolita*. He later said he found Brando to be more than a little disingenuous in his dealings, and Peckinpah had nothing good to say about the finished product. The screenplay credit went to Guy Trosper, whom Brando had hired on, and Willingham, though Brando declared that he rewrote virtually all of the script himself with Trosper. Various biographers of Peckinpah and Brando have written that the screenplay bore little or no resemblance to the one crafted by Peckinpah, but I've read his screenplay and it compares favorably to the final version except for the crucial point of making out Malden's character, Dad Longworth, to be a liar along with everybody else. Brando said he lost interest in the film in the editing stage and just let Paramount cut the picture to their satisfaction. Who's lying here? It is incomprehensible to me that Peckinpah was not accorded a credit for the screenplay. By 1973, when he directed *Pat Garrett and Billy the Kid*, his own lethargy doomed the project. (As Jim Hamilton, who worked on the script of *Cross of Iron* [1977] said, "*Pat Garrett and Billy the Kid* was one of the most fatigue-ridden movies ever made.") It's too bad that Peckinpah couldn't trump Brando with his own treatment of the same subject, but the truth is that *One-Eyed Jacks* is a better film than *Pat Garrett and Billy the Kid*, a lot better. Kubrick never did make a Western.

9. Don't Forget to Thank the Producer

Frank Rosenberg, the producer of *One-Eyed Jacks*, died on my birthday, October 18, in 2002. A well-known actor once asked me, only semirhetorically, "What does a producer do?" Most people not intimate with the movie business think that the producer raises the money to get the picture made, and in most cases this is true. But producers do many things having nothing (or everything) to do with money. They cast, write (and rewrite), fetch, pamper, persuade, murder, organize, disturb, finagle, fade away, bully, mollycoddle (I've always wanted to use that word), and, if they're really smart, stay out of the way once the ball has begun to roll. Producers such as David O. Selznick (*Gone with the Wind*, *Duel in the Sun*, etc.) stood in the middle of the road doing everything imaginable. Others just let the director, actors, cameraman, and so on do the job they were hired to do.

It was Frank Rosenberg who hired Sam Peckinpah to write the first draft of *One-Eyed Jacks*. This is significant because it was the very first time Peckinpah had tried his hand at scripting a feature-length film. Rosenberg also gave Jayne Mansfield her start in motion pictures (he obviously understood the meaning of the word *motion*), in *Illegal* in 1955, with Edward G. Robinson and Nina Foch. Here was a producer with an eye for talent—Peckinpah, of course—but Mansfield had talent, too. She was a terrific comedian—dig *Will Success Spoil Rock Hunter?* for example. Under the tutelage of a director like Frank Tashlin, she thrived.

Born in Brooklyn soon after the turn of the twentieth century, Frank Rosenberg went to work at sixteen in the shipping department of Columbia Pictures in New York. Columbia's czar, Harry Cohn, tabbed him to run his national publicity and advertising department. In his early forties, Rosenberg moved to Hollywood to helm the Columbia publicity office there, and a few years later he struck out on his own, producing films for Warner Brothers, Twentieth Century Fox, Columbia, and others. I'll always be indebted to him for producing *King of the Khyber Rifles*, starring Tyrone Power, one of my favorite childhood films. I saw *King of the Khyber Rifles* at the Ciné theater in Chicago in 1953 with my father, who called the star Tyrone Cupcake. My dad did not think highly of most movie stars as human beings. Watching Ty Cupcake as a half-caste British officer commanding Indian cavalry riding against Afghan hordes did not inspire my father to change his opinion. In his business he'd dealt with a lot of Hollywood types, he knew their habits and tendencies and how phony they were, but he didn't spoil my fantasy—not yet, anyway.

Back to Frank Rosenberg. According to Rosenberg, it was he who bought the rights to Charles Neider's novel

The Authentic Death of Hendry Jones, perhaps at Brando's request. In any case, his first writing hire was Rod Serling, creator of the fabulously successful television series *The Twilight Zone*. Serling did an adaptation of the novel, which Rosenberg rejected, and he then turned to Peckinpah. Bloody Sam did a better job and Brando went for it right away, but as we know, once Marlon's pudgy fingers got into the goo, Peckinpah was soon removed from the mix.

The important part of all this is to remember that Rosenberg got the movie made. He did what he had to do even if it meant spooning *menudo* down Marlon Cupcake's throat or getting the seamstress to let out his pants a little (or a lot). Frank Rosenberg also produced the detective drama *Madigan* in 1968 with Richard Widmark, a considerably thinner actor.

In Search of the City of Ghosts

Sixteen years ago, I was sitting at home watching a ballgame on TV with my daughter, Phoebe, who was then fifteen, when the telephone rang.

It was the young actor Matt Dillon, star of the recent films *The Flamingo Kid*, *The Outsiders*, *Rumble Fish*, etc., calling to tell me he had just finished reading my novel *Port Tropique*. He liked it very much, he said, and he was interested in portraying the protagonist in a movie version. I told him that the film rights had been sold, a script was being developed, and I appreciated his interest. A problem for Matt was that the main character in the novel was in his late forties and he was only twenty-two. I didn't think it could work. Wait a few years, I said, and if the film hasn't been made, we can talk about it again. We chatted a bit—he and his manager, Vic Ramos, were in Lawrence, Kansas, shooting a movie—and then I offered the phone to my daughter, who screamed when I told her Matt Dillon, the teenage heartthrob, was on the line. Phoebe was too nonplussed to speak to him, seeing as how he was one of her cinematic heroes, and so, after he'd given me his telephone number in New York, I thanked him again for his interest and hung up.

As it happened, the film of *Port Tropique* was never made (though Matt still talks about doing it), and, as the years passed, Matt and Vic and I became good friends. I saw Matt when I was in New York, we went together to dinner, bars, jazz clubs; and he visited with me and my family (Phoebe calmed down) when he was in San Francisco. In fact, Phoebe and I were with Matt in New York in the apartment he lives in now just after he'd bought it and it was still empty. It was there that, several years later, we would begin writing the screenplay for the first film Matt would direct, *City of Ghosts*.

Matt told me that he had grown increasingly dissatisfied with the quality of the scripts he was being offered. He also felt that, after almost twenty years of acting in movies, he had a desire to be more proactive, to write and direct, to put to use the additional skills and lessons he had acquired by working with such talented directors as Francis Ford Coppola, Gus Van Sant, Tim Hunter, and others. Matt comes from a family of artists: his great-uncle, Alex Raymond, created the comic book character Flash Gordon; and his father, Paul, is an accomplished portrait painter. Though Matt's formal education ended when he was fourteen, I was always impressed by his sincere, probing, and continuing interest in the arts, encompassing music, painting, photography, and literature. Having perused several of Matt's sketchbooks, I could tell by his marks that he, too, possessed a deft hand and eye. It did not surprise me that Matt not only wanted more control over his film projects but that he also had a passion to create.

It was in 1996, soon after I had written with director David Lynch the screenplay for *Lost Highway* that Matt called me and said he wanted to direct a movie. He had taken a trip to Vietnam, Laos, and Cambodia and been fascinated by these countries. Let's write a story that could be filmed there, he said. Oddly enough, he and I had both read around the same time an item in the *International Herald Tribune* identifying Cambodia as a sanctuary for more than three hundred international fugitives, due to the fact of Cambodia's never having signed extradition treaties with any other countries. Criminals on the run could find a safe harbor in Cambodia so long as they could afford to live there. If you can pay, you can stay, was Cambodia's policy. Just as Robert Vesco had done in Cuba for so many years. Most of the fugitives in Cambodia, we read, were Chinese; but there were men and women on the run from Canada, the United States, France, almost everywhere. To call Cambodia a safe haven, however, was a stretch—the country itself was hardly free of dangers. It seemed an ideal place to set a story filled with tension and intrigue.

I told Matt I'd think about it, and soon thereafter remembered Joseph Conrad's novel *An Outcast of the Islands*, which had long interested me as film material. Conrad's story of an Englishman adrift in the wilds of Malaysia, cut off physically and spiritually from his own society, had fascinated me since I had first read it at the age of eighteen. I wanted to know how and why a person privy to "all the advantages" of a so-called civilized world could abandon himself completely in the Land of the Unknown. Carol Reed, the British director, had made a film based on the novel in the early 1950s, and I told Matt about it. He obtained a video of the movie and we watched it together. We shared an admiration for both Reed and the story, and agreed that it could be an inspiration for what we were planning to do, combined with the news item.

Matt also had another story involving a super swindle that had gone down in Southeast Asia to add to the mix, and so we spent five days in his apartment knocking out a screen treatment for him to present to a pair of French producers who were interested in backing the development of the script. The French guys liked our plan and came up with the money to get us started writing the screenplay. It didn't matter that Matt had not directed a feature film before—he had directed some music videos, and would, before undertaking the enormous task of piloting *City of Ghosts*, direct an episode of the HBO TV series *Oz*—if we could write a good screenplay, the French producers reasoned, the rest would take care of itself.

It had taken David Lynch and myself two months to write the screenplay for *Lost Highway*. David had done the film adaptation of my novel *Wild at Heart* in approximately one week. I had written the first draft of the screenplay based on my novel *Perdita Durango* in three weeks. (It was filmed in 1997 by the Spanish director Alex de la Iglesia.) I was willing to devote a couple of months to Matt's and my project. Four years later, after having written together in New York, Miami, Sicily, Rome, San Francisco, and I forget where else, Mattie and I had what we felt was a script worth shooting. We had not, of course, worked steadily for all this time, each having pursued other projects in order to keep eating; but *City of Ghosts* was always there, waiting for us, bedeviling us, fascinating us, challenging us. The story kept changing—plot, characters, even location—but despite and even because of our individual and collective frustrations and disagreements, we won the battle. The screenplay was done. Now we had to get the money to make the movie. The French producers were out of both francs and patience—not necessarily in that order. They were good guys, but funding a screenplay and bankrolling a feature film are two very different animals. Francis Coppola once told me, "Getting the money for the small check," he said, meaning for the screenplay, "pardon me, but that's nothing. Just try getting someone to write the *big* check, for the production. *That's* the tough one."

It took another few months to put together the financing, and in the end MGM/United Artists thought enough of the package—by this time the actors James Caan, Gérard Depardieu, Natascha McElhone, and Stellan Skarsgård, among others, had signed on—to guarantee domestic distribution. Each of the principal actors expressed an immediate affection for both the story we had concocted and the prospect of being on location in a mysterious place. James Caan had never before been to Asia, so for him it was a genuine adventure. And Gérard Depardieu was, perhaps, the most daring of all, having undergone, only a couple of weeks prior to the start of filming, quintuple heart bypass surgery. Depardieu arrived in Cambodia carrying only an extra pair of pants and a toothbrush. "I always travel light," he said.

The difficult part was that Matt was determined to film almost exclusively in Cambodia, where no feature had been made since *Lord Jim* in the 1960s, and even then they shot only two weeks in the country. Matt stuck to his guns and his vision and somehow, miraculously, got it done his way. Mostly. Mostly means a lot when you're working with a limited budget. All budgets are limited, of course, but some are more limited than others. Matt fought for what he wanted, shooting in some obscure regions of Cambodia such as Kampot and Udon. Cambodia itself is a character in *City of Ghosts*, and the true hero of the film is portrayed by a former nonactor, a Cambodian cyclo driver whom Matt discovered in Phnom Penh. And the city referred to in the title is both a mysterious, metaphorical one and a literal city, New York, a place to which the fugitives can no longer return, a lost city whose inhabitants are now as good as ghosts for them, a city to be returned to only in memory and dreams.

City of Ghosts is filled with exotica but rooted in the harsh reality of what happens when a search for a new beginning collides with greed and delusion. Matt and I sent the protagonist, Jimmy Cremmins, on a pilgrimage to reclaim himself, both in body and soul, and to get to where he's going he must pass through shadows and darkness, the dogs of doubt biting his heels. And Matt Dillon, as director, cowriter, and actor was on a pilgrimage of his own, an ambitious excursion for which he should be given proper credit and allowed a certain amount of grace. He's earned it, in my opinion, and put something on the big screen that he—and I—can be proud of.

At the conclusion of a screening of *City of Ghosts* at the Toronto Film Festival last September, during the question and answer session, an Asian woman stood up and addressed Matt, Stellan, and myself. She said that she and a contingent of South Asian people had come to view the film to see if the depiction of people and place was exploitative and/or inaccurate. She told us that their reaction was one of relief and even admiration. Despite the violence and tawdry circumstances in parts of the movie, they felt that we had treated the Cambodian culture and social situations with respect and even tenderness. There was nothing in the film, she said, to which they would object. Matt thanked her for her comments, and then Stellan asked, "But did you like it?" "Yes!" she answered, smiling now. "It was very exciting!" After five years, our search was over.

Fuzzy Sandwiches, or There Is No Speed Limit on the Lost Highway

In 1995, when David Lynch, who had directed the film version of my novel *Wild at Heart*, and also had directed my two plays, *Tricks* and *Blackout*, for a television production entitled *Hotel Room*, came to me and asked me to write with him the screenplay for a new film, I could hardly say no. After all, *Wild at Heart* had won the Palme d'Or at the Cannes Film Festival and propelled the book onto best seller lists all over the world. Besides, we were good friends by then. The problem was that I was busily engaged writing a novel and was scheduled to leave for Spain in two weeks. How could we get a screenplay done *right now*? as Dave asked. In fact, he insisted. So I put aside the novel manuscript and agreed to work hard for two weeks and see what we came up with. If it seemed to be working after my return from Spain, if we both felt good about the project, then we would continue and work straight through until we had it finished.

David had optioned for film my novel *Night People*, and we had talked for a year or more about how it could be done, but nothing had happened. (He told me his daughter, Jennifer, wanted to play the role of one of the two lesbian serial killers.) He fell in love with a couple of sentences in the book in particular, one of which was when one woman says to another, "We're just a couple of Apaches ridin' wild on the lost highway." What did it mean? he wanted to know. What was the *deeper* meaning of the phrase "lost highway"? He had an idea for a story. What if one day a person woke up and he was another person? An entirely different person from the person he had been the day before. Okay, I said, that's Kafka, *The Metamorphosis*. But we did not want this person to turn into an insect. So that's what we had to start with: a title, *Lost Highway*; a sentence from close to the end of *Night People* ("You and me, mister, we can really out-ugly them sumbitches, can't we?"); the notion of irrefutable change; and a vision Dave had about someone receiving videotapes of his life from an unknown source, something he had thought of following the wrap of the shooting of *Twin Peaks: Fire Walk with Me*. Now all we had to do was make a coherent story out of this.

A few years ago, when David, the producer Monty Montgomery, my friend Vinnie Deserio, and I were sitting around talking about another story, Dave, in an effort to explain to me an effect he was after, said, "You know that feeling you get when you've just gotten back from the dry cleaners a pair of slacks, Dacron slacks, and you reach your hand in a pocket and you feel those *fuzzy sandwiches* with your fingers? Well, that's the feeling

I'm looking for." I just nodded and replied, "Okay, Dave, I know *exactly* what you mean."

I kept this incident in mind while he and I sat across from one another and puzzled out the scenario for *Lost Highway*, which I like to call "Orpheus and Eurydice Meet *Double Indemnity*." We made it work—at least for each other—and I love the result, fuzzy sandwiches and all. That being said, it's important to understand that David and I work similarly—very hard, long hours, with time out only for coffee—in Dave's case, *lots of coffee*. Working with Dave is, for me, a great treat, because I know that as the director he's going to add an extra dimension to whatever we come up with on the page. Visually, it will take one giant step beyond. This gives me the confidence to let everything loose, a great privilege for a writer.

Both Lynch and I believe that films are, or should be, like dreams. When you enter the movie theater the "real" world is shut out. Now you are in the thrall of the filmmakers, you *must* surrender and allow the film's images to wash over you, to drown in them for two hours or so. And David is relentless in his use of imagery. *Lost Highway*, like *Blue Velvet* or *Eraserhead*, especially, is filled with unforgettable images. And we are set in a place, a city, a landscape, that is neither here nor there, a timeless form, presented within a nonlinear structure—a Möbius strip, curling back and under, running parallel to itself before again becoming connected, only there's a kind of coda— but that's how it goes with psychogenic fugues. Figure it out for yourself, you'll feel better later; and if you don't figure it out, you'll feel even *better*, trust us. Trust is what it's all about with filmmakers like David Lynch, one of the very, very few true visionaries in the history of cinema. I once asked David, who is a painter, why he decided to make movies, and he told me (echoing many others, including Elia Kazan, who said, "The camera is such a beautiful instrument. It paints with motion"), "Because I wanted to see my paintings move."

Vinnie Deserio once said that the reason Dave and I work so well together is that he takes the ordinary and makes it seem extraordinary, and I take the extraordinary and make it seem ordinary. Maybe so; it sounds goods, anyway. But there are no easy explanations for what occurs in *Lost Highway* or *Eraserhead*, nor should there be. When you go on a journey with David Lynch, it's a trip you've never been on before—and may never want to take again—but it's unforgettable. Time to fasten your seat belt, as Bette Davis so memorably instructed (words by Joseph Mankiewicz) in *All About Eve*, because there is no speed limit on the lost highway.

Keeper of the Cat People
A Paean to Val Lewton

―――――

I grew up mostly in hotels, traveling with my mother during the 1950s from Chicago to Miami and Key West, Florida; New Orleans, Louisiana; Jackson, Mississippi; Havana, Cuba; and elsewhere. I was very often left alone at night and I spent a lot of time watching old movies on television. It was during this period that I discovered the films of Val Lewton, the producer and sometime screenwriter (using the names Carlos Keith and Cosmo Forbes, among others). I was probably eight or nine years old when I first saw *Cat People* and *Curse of the Cat People* on an all-night movie channel in Chicago.

Watching these masterpieces of chiaroscuro at 3 A.M. made an indelible impression on me. These were horror films unlike any others. As the director Martin Scorsese has remarked, they were "wonderfully inventive, beautifully poetic, and deeply unsettling ... some of the greatest treasures we have."

With films such as *The Leopard Man*, *I Walked with a Zombie*, *The Body Snatcher*, *Bedlam*, *The Seventh Victim*, and *Isle of the Dead*, Lewton created an oeuvre unique in film history. Using shadows to disguise the grisly goings-on (always in black-and-white) and the power of suggestion—never revealing for viewers' eyes the graphic activities we only hear or see reflected on walls or in water—Lewton's terrifying formula set one's imagination stumbling down a street where the light is always hazy, the black not quite black but with an opaqueness that forces the viewer to strain to see more clearly. The effect is like looking through a keyhole and being shocked by a cold fingertip on your neck.

Before Val Lewton made movies, he was a novelist, producing nine more or less conventional works, plus one book of pornography, *Yasmine* (or *Grushenskaya*). The re-publication of his Depression-era novel, *No Bed of Her Own*, originally issued by the Vanguard Press in New York in 1932, gives those of us familiar with Lewton's films an opportunity to experience his long-out-of-print efforts at writing fiction, and brings again to light his fascinating work behind the camera.

No Bed of Her Own is a straightforward tale of an out-of-work young woman in New York City during the depths of the Great Depression—1931, to be exact. Fired from her job as a stenographer in an office, Rose Mahoney goes from respectable (if somewhat irresponsible) to the lower depths, doing whatever it takes to stay alive, including prostitution. She's not a bad girl, however, and novelist Lewton keeps us aware of her standards. As Lewton's son, Val E. Lewton, writes in the preface to the new edition, Rose's "standards, admirably frank and genuine, don't cut it in a world without work. Like Micawber in *David Copperfield*, Rose keeps expecting that something will turn up."

Written in a style similar to Edward Anderson's *Hungry Men* or B. Traven's *The Cotton-Pickers*, *No Bed of Her Own* (titled by Lewton's wife) details Rose's travails step by step down the ladder of degradation. Yes, it's a story of greed and desire, of man's inhumanity to man, a novel with a message (although my guess is that Lewton probably subscribed to the oft-quoted sentiment that if you want to send a message, go to Western Union); after all, the 1930s was a desperate time in America, a period during which many artists and intellectuals joined the Communist party or became fellow travelers. Rose's story ends melodramatically, tragically, but she survives. The reader doesn't know what will happen to her, but Lewton makes us care; that is his triumph. (The novel was bought by Paramount as a vehicle for Miriam Hopkins but never filmed.)

Val Lewton was born Vladimir Ivan Leventon in Yalta, Russia, in 1904. He was Jewish, the son of a ne'er-do-well moneylender named Max Hofschneider and Nina Leventon, a pharmacist's daughter. In 1909, following a two-year interlude in Berlin, Nina and her son emigrated to the United States, where they lived with Nina's younger sister, the former Adelaida Leventon, who, having gone to America several years earlier, had reinvented herself as Alla Nazimova, the actress and socialite, famous for her successes on Broadway in plays by Ibsen and Chekhov (a friend in the old country) and for her society parties. She was also infamous for her lesbian bacchanals.

The freshly dubbed Val Lewton studied for a time at Columbia University and then worked as a journalist. He was fired from his job as a reporter for the *Darien-Stamford Review* after it was discovered that a story he'd written about a truckload of kosher chickens dying in a New York heat wave was a fabrication. It was through Nazimova that he eventually found his way to Hollywood. His mother went to work in the story department of Metro (later MGM) in New York, thanks to her sister, and got Val a job in the publicity department. By this time, 1928, he had published two novels.

He continued to write books, and left Metro after a short time, but when Nina was contacted by the producer David O. Selznick and asked to provide him with a scriptwriter for his projected film *Taras Bulba* (never made), she suggested her own son, one of whose novels was a Russian potboiler entitled *The Cossack Sword*. So Lewton emigrated farther west, to California, where he worked in various capacities for Selznick for eight years on films including *Gone with the Wind*, *Rebecca*, *A Star Is Born*, and *A Tale of Two Cities*.

In 1942, Lewton went to work at RKO Pictures, a company nearly bankrupted by the financial failures of Orson Welles's masterworks, *Citizen Kane* and *The Magnificent Ambersons*. Lewton was signed on to produce a series of low-budget horror films, and the rest is history.

He enlisted the film cutters Robert Wise and Mark Robson to direct his productions. Both had worked with Welles, Wise having edited, with Robson's assistance, *Kane* and *Ambersons* (for which Wise also directed additional scenes that were cut into the film without Welles's permission). Robson edited *Cat People* and directed five Lewton films; Wise directed three Lewton pictures and later made such classics as *The Day the Earth Stood Still*, *Odds Against Tomorrow*, *West Side Story*, and *The Sound of Music*.

Lewton's *Cat People*, based on a story by DeWitt Bodeen, saved RKO. For a while he was their hero, albeit an irascible one. Arguably his finest partnership was with Jacques Tourneur, who had worked with Lewton at Metro and directed *Cat People*, *I Walked with a Zombie*, and *The Leopard Man*. As long as Lewton stuck to horror fare, he was successful; his other productions, such as *Mademoiselle Fifi* (directed by Wise), *Youth Runs Wild* (directed by Robson) and *Apache Drums* (his final film, in 1951), did not live up to the studio's expectations. Lewton's nuanced, cultured scary pictures of the 1940s were championed by James Agee, who lauded Lewton's work in his film commentaries in *Time* and *The Nation*. His movies cast a spell over the viewer, who was invited into a dream world where submission is tantamount to giving yourself over to a leering hypnotist and his hunchbacked dwarf henchman named Arg.

It's *The Seventh Victim* (1943), Lewton's eerie movie about a New York City–based witch cult, that seems to me most closely allied to *No Bed of Her Own*. Here again is the girl adrift, frightened and lost, forced around dark corners, powerless yet somehow brave and daring. In his expert afterword appended to the novel, Damien Love states that the theme of *No Bed of Her Own* "is the underlying theme of all Lewton's movies from *Cat People* on; how life can shift a fraction of a degree, shadows come rushing, and people can find themselves slipping into a world whose existence they never suspected."

Val Lewton was not really happy in Hollywood. He was foremost a literary man: in LA he hired John Fante to write scripts and befriended William Faulkner, Thomas Mann, and Christopher Isherwood. In the film business he had to move among philistines, creatures antagonistic to those of artistic temperament; but, even though Lewton died young, from a heart attack at the age of forty-six, in 1951, he was able to articulate his vision to the extent that more than half a century later his work continues to entrance, provoke, and beguile.

Confidential as a Baby's Cry

Call Northside 777 was a nifty little black-and-white crime film made in mock-documentary style by director Henry Hathaway in 1948. Starring James Stewart, Richard Conte, and Lee J. Cobb, it tracked a cynical Chicago newspaper reporter (Stewart) as he uncovered the facts necessary to spring from prison a man (Conte) falsely convicted for murdering a cop in a speakeasy. Based on an actual case, *Call Northside 777* (a telephone number) established Chicago as a character in the story, much as the A&E television series *City Confidential* uses cities and towns as disparate as Gibsonton, Florida, Los Angeles, California, Ruthton, Minnesota, Miami, Florida, and Skidmore, Missouri, making them central to the plot. It's a successful device. Each one-hour episode follows the formula of history of place plus present-day (or almost) world gone wrong, featuring a mysterious murder.

The use of the word *confidential* in the context of exposé was worked to death in the early 1950s, most notably in the vulgar investigative books by Jack Lait and Lee Mortimer, which team produced *Chicago Confidential* (1950), *New York Confidential! The Big City After Dark*

(1951), *Washington Confidential* (1952), and the perhaps overly ambitious *USA Confidential* (1952). These guilty reads ransacked newspaper files for stories of racketeers and gun molls and dirty politicians, much as cheap magazines of the day, such as *True Detective*, did, banking on the public's fascination for lurid if not specious (let alone facetious) yarns. Phil Karlson made a solid caper picture in 1952 called *Kansas City Confidential*, but it was his 1955 movie, the so-called docudrama *The Phenix City Story*, that (whether the show's creators know it or not) really is the granddaddy of *City Confidential*. (And don't forget crooner Sonny Knight's 1960s teen ballad, "Confidential," from which my title is taken.)

The Phenix City Story was based on the exploits of John Patterson, then attorney general of the state of Alabama (he later became governor), who made his reputation by "cleaning up" the vice-ridden town of Phenix City, which is located on the Georgia-Alabama line. Offering the usual array of divertissements, viz., prostitution, gambling, cheap liquor, catering to the soldiers spilling across the border from Fort Benning, Phenix City made headlines all over the country thanks to the crusading John Patterson, whom Karlson made out to be a heroic figure. The truth was something less, of course—especially when it came to Patterson's stance on civil rights—but something less than the truth is standard when it comes to an exercise as imprecise as docudrama.

Using digital video, *City Confidential* brings the viewer into the moment, almost as if it were a well-made home video. Sure, some of the images are repetitious or seemingly unrelated to the events at hand, but there is an intimacy in the way this is done that is ingenuous and intriguing, creating the feeling that we may suddenly glimpse something completely unexpected and/or shocking. The mood is colorfully enhanced by the voice-over narration provided by Paul Winfield, an Academy Award nominee for best actor (*Sounder*, 1972), and Emmy Award winner (*Picket Fences*). Sounding alternately laconic, arch, and even patrician, Winfield's recitation of the text provided for him by the program's writers is replete with tongue-in-cheek (I presume) hard lefts and cute rights, such as these from the Gibsonton, Florida, episode about carnival freaks, focusing on the slaying of Grady Stiles Jr., known because of his malformed hands and feet as "Lobster Boy": "It's never over 'til the bearded fat lady sings" and "Two of the hands clapping were claws." The show on Los Angeles, which details the killing of a strip club entrepreneur named Horace "Big Mac" McKenna, a convicted counterfeiter and swindler (credit card fraud), is chockablock with stale lines even Mickey Spillane would have tossed, among the worst being: "The news blew through like a sailor with a pocketful of greenbacks." The segment set in Ozark, Arkansas, about the murder of a flamboyant female doctor endowed with "an enormous breast augmentation," employs these throwaways: "Sunk . . . faster than beer cans in the Arkansas River" and ". . . tougher to stomach than the cube steak at the Ozark Inn."

This kind of purposeful purpling of the lingo is never condescending or mean. It's fun, and it sounds as if Paul Winfield is getting a kick out of saying the lines, too. Episodes set in small, seemingly peaceful towns begin with the tease, "... a very unique community. The last place you would expect a murder." We are at once transported to Jim Thompson territory. Author of many paperback original tours de force, most published in the 1950s, such as *The Killer Inside Me, Pop. 1280, The Alcoholics,* and *The Getaway,* Thompson, who grew up in the dust bowl town of Anadarko, Oklahoma, peppered his novels with the same kind of corny metaphors and silly descriptions (Horace McKenna, the LA strip club king, worked in the "titillation trade") employed by the *City Confidential* scripters. Paul Winfield's grave (and occasionally graveyard) delivery allows us to wade through the trash without actually getting intellectually icky; absent Mr. Winfield, I'm afraid, *City Confidential* would be more in the realm of the lower-rent program *Cops.* If not satire to the level of Juvenal, *City Confidential* does at least wander in that direction.

Of the episodes I've watched, the one that impressed me most was set in Skidmore, Missouri. This 1981 case of a vigilante group disposing by shotguns of a town bully, Ken Rex McElroy, called "the barbarian of Nodaway County," was skillfully and seriously put together. The use of interviews of citizens of Skidmore combined with a mountain of factual information on McElroy detailing his personal history, which included having been the fifteenth of sixteen children, an irredeemable thief of livestock, corn, grain, liquor, etc., unapologetic brutalizer of his several wives and fifteen children (he blew off the chin of his first wife with a shotgun), was genuinely compelling. Everyone in Skidmore and the surrounding area really hated this guy, and when the police couldn't take care of the problem, the people did. Ken Rex was shot to death after having imbibed six beers while he sat in his pickup truck in front of the D&G Bar in the middle of town one weekday morning. Nobody would divulge the names of the triggermen or women. When McElroy's widow filed a six-million-dollar wrongful death lawsuit against the townsfolk, her house was burned to the ground. Though there was proof of arson, nobody was arrested for the crime. After that, she and her children moved away and the suit was dropped. Jim Thompson would have had a ball with this one.

I wouldn't necessarily describe watching *City Confidential* as a guilty pleasure. It's too self-aware for that. The fact that the program operates on a modest budget and rakes up sensational cases from the past does not disqualify it from being not only entertaining but, as with the segment on Skidmore, sometimes meaningful, the same way certain noir or hard-boiled writers such as Thompson, David Goodis, Charles Williams, and others mined the lives of the tortured and forgotten in order to examine more closely (and often more feverishly) the human condition. My ideal viewing companion for *City*

Confidential would be William Faulkner. I can imagine Mr. Bill, as many citizens of his hometown, Oxford, Mississippi, still refer to him, taking a long sip of sour mash whiskey, pointing at the television set, and drawling, "I might could have used that bit in *Sanctuary*."

Souvenir of Evil

A few years ago, I viewed an exhibit on the history of tattoos at a small museum in Flims, a village in the Swiss Alps. The first two floors housed predictable displays of photographs of a variety of body decoration, from tattooing to piercing, along with video monitors featuring practitioners of these arts expounding on method, motive, and desire. The third floor contained similar displays, but one area was partitioned off, dimly lit, with a separate doorway. In this room was a lamp covered by a shade made out of human skin. The skin, prior to having been flayed, I presume, had been tattooed with the words "Sancta Maria" and an illustration of a girl's face. A card explained that this item was created during the 1930s or '40s in Germany. It was on loan from a private collection in the United States.

Of course I had heard about the Nazis making lampshades from the skin of Jews and others they had murdered in their concentration camps, but I had never before seen the evidence, nor had I ever expected to. I was with two friends, the Swiss film and opera director Daniel Schmid and his assistant, Christophe. The three of us were the only ones present in this section of the museum, and each of us was shocked and horrified in ways we had difficulty describing. Daniel, who had read about the exhibit in a local newspaper, said that no mention of this particular object had been made in the article. Christophe, who is in his early twenties, asked me if I thought appropriate that such a horror be displayed for the public. I couldn't answer. He suggested that if this were done in America protestors would demonstrate in front of the building. I thought there should perhaps be a warning sign outside this small room apprising people of what they would witness inside, a souvenir of evil.

Before leaving the building, I mentioned to the middle-aged Swiss woman stationed at the entrance desk that I thought some museum-goers might find offensive the display of a lampshade made out of human skin, let alone skin taken from concentration camp victims. She expressed surprise at my remark. "Why should anyone be offended?" she replied. "It's part of the history of this subject."

After I returned to California, where I live, I related to my friend Ira, a former Israeli commando, what I had seen. He told me he thought it was good to have such a thing available for public consumption, so that people would be reminded of the Holocaust, especially in light of ongoing strife in the Middle East. Then Ira told me the following joke.

Bush, Sharon, and Putin meet to discuss the conflict between the Jews and the Arabs in an effort to resolve the problem, but they can find no way to alleviate the crisis. God appears and tells them He's disgusted with the whole thing. He has decided to destroy mankind and take a break. Maybe, He says, in the future, He'll take another crack at it and start again. Then, God disappears.

Bush goes back to the United States and addresses the people. He tells them he has good news and bad news. The good news is that there is a God; the bad news is He is going to destroy mankind. Putin goes back to Russia and tells his people that he has bad news and terrible news. The bad news is that there is a God; and the terrible news is that He is going to destroy mankind. Sharon goes back to Israel and tells the Israelis that he has good news and wonderful news. The good news is that there is a God; but the wonderful news is that there will never, ever be a state of Palestine.

"That joke could also be told from a Palestinian perspective," I said. "Sure," said Ira, "but it came from the mind of an Israeli."

I thought about the tattooed skin on the lampshade and remembered that, according to Jewish tradition, tattoos were considered taboo. Perhaps the skin was not taken from a Jew (more likely a Gypsy), but of course it doesn't matter. When I was a boy in Chicago, the only people I knew who had tattoos were either sailors or Jewish survivors of concentration camps who had numbers burned into their arms by the Nazis. The Nazis certainly knew of the Jewish prohibition on tattoos. My father, who was Jewish and a racketeer, told me never to get a tattoo. If I had one, he said, I could always be identified, and there might come a day when I would prefer not to be. That made sense, so I've never gotten a tattoo.

The more I think about the joke Ira told me, the more I like it. If God destroyed mankind, would it matter? No more than whether the skin on the lampshade was taken from a Jew, because nobody would be around to even consider the question.

Sailor & Lula and the Capital R

"What's that you're eyeballin', Peanut?"

"Book of photos of works of modern art Beany sent me for my birthday—which is the day after tomorrow, case you didn't remember yet to buy me them teardrop earrings I been hintin' at so hard."

Sailor Ripley, who had just gotten home from his job at the Gator Gone reptile repellent factory, plopped down in his Barcalounger in the den of his and Lula's house in Metairie, Louisiana. He took a swig from the bottle of Abita Amber he was holding in his right hand and held out his left.

"Pass it over, Lula," he said, "let me have a look."

"Oh, Sailor, you just gonna make fun of these pictures like you do every time you see some paintin' or sculpture or movie challenges your concept of reality."

"My reality been challenged more'n a few times, baby, you know it. I ain't always been up for it, I'll admit, which is why I been inside the walls back in the day, but studyin' the type of art with a capital R do give me a good laugh now and again."

Lula slammed the book shut, stood up from the bamboo loveseat she'd been perched on and stared at her husband.

"You always makin' fun of things you don't understand," she said. "As many things as there are I love about you, Sailor, that's one part I don't. Just 'cause another person's mind works different than yours don't mean what he or she creates ain't worth thinkin' on or appreciatin'."

"Hand it here, honey. Let me give it a try."

Lula handed the book to Sailor. He set down his beer on a side table, opened the book and turned the pages for a bit, then stopped.

"Now here's one does make some sense," he said.

Lula came around the back of the Barcalounger and looked over Sailor's left shoulder.

"What is it?"

"Called 'Black and White Disaster,'" said Sailor. "Same picture over and over like on the strip of photos you get if you don't move around over to the four-for-a-quarter booth in front of the Winn-Dixie."

"It's a paintin' by Andy Warhol," Lula said. "Maybe followin' a car wreck, man carryin' a woman's body."

"Could she jumped out of a window and he scraped up her corpse off the sidewalk."

"Oh, Sail, you always got the goriest imagination."

"Not exactly sure why the picture's gotta be repeated, let's see, twenty-five times, though."

"That's what you call the capital R part," said Lula.

She walked back over to the bamboo loveseat, picked up her cigarettes and lighter, and fired up a More.

"Weren't this Warhol the one wore a bad wig, got famous for paintin' a soup can, then got shot by a deranged female up in New York?"

"That's the one," said Lula. "She didn't kill him, though. He died later of somethin' else. Now his paintin's sell for millions of dollars."

"I lose any more hair, Lula, I'm gonna have to start wearin' a wig my own self."

"Toupee, baby, it's called a toupee. You want, we could cover up that bald spot you have right now with a little Sultan of Africa shoe polish."

Sailor closed the book, picked up his Abita and took a long swallow.

"He got death right, though."

"What you mean?" asked Lula.

"Dead is dead, peanut. I guess that's why the pictures is all the same. Ain't nothin' can change it."

Lula smiled.

"Why, Sail, honey," she said, "there might could be more to you than meets the eye."

MUSIC

The Last Time I Saw Artie

Artie Shaw, the clarinetist and bandleader, died in 2005 at the age of ninety-four. Born Arthur Arshawsky in New York City and raised there and in New Haven, Connecticut, he lived the last third of his life in Newbury Park, California, near Thousand Oaks, which is where I met him in 1982. The reason for our meeting was to talk about the writer William Saroyan, who had died the year before, and about whom my associate Larry Lee and I were writing a biography. Artie had introduced Saroyan to Carol Marcus, whom the Academy Award– and Pulitzer Prize–winning author had married twice. (After her second divorce from Saroyan, Carol went on to marry Walter Matthau, to whom she remained married for the rest of her life.)

Shaw, a tall, balding man with a bushy mustache, greeted Larry and me in the driveway of his modest house. "Hey, you remind me of the young Jimmy Caan," he said to me. Artie was seventy then; with him at his house was his twenty-nine-year-old girlfriend, a former music student of his. He seemed very strong. In his heyday, the 1930s and '40s, Shaw, along with his rival Benny Goodman, was the most famous bandleader in America. He made headlines by hiring an African American vocalist—Billie Holiday—the first white bandleader to do so, as well as for his groundbreaking orchestral arrangements; but his greatest notoriety came as a result of his eight marriages.

Among Artie Shaw's wives were the actresses Ava Gardner, Lana Turner, and Evelyn Keyes; and the best-selling author Kathleen Winsor, who looked like a movie star. Artie told me his eight marriages lasted a real-time total of four years. "Six months together," he said, "and six months to get the divorce." I asked him why the marriages failed. "After six months," he explained, "the Artie Shaw mask came off; so did the Lana Turner and Ava Gardner masks. Then we were stuck with the real person, which was too frightening to contemplate, so the deal was off. We ran away from each other."

Shaw was a big star; he even appeared in a few films, usually as himself.

"The reason I married these women had to do with access," he told us. "I'd walk into the Stork Club in New York and Sherman Billingsley, the owner, would immediately usher me into the Cub Room in the back, where celebrities could have privacy and not be hassled by the hoi polloi. I'd sit down next to Judy Garland, or Lana, or Ava, or Rita Hayworth. We'd strike up a conversation and make a date. It was like the high school cafeteria, only all the girls were beautiful."

I told Artie that of the women he'd married, the one I preferred was Ava Gardner. "Yeah, Ava was okay," he said, "but you shoulda seen Lana at eighteen with that blond mane in a convertible. Boy, was she something. For a Jewish kid like me, she was the ultimate shiksa. None of us was perfectly behaved, but Lana in particular liked to be admired. I remember when she was making *The Postman Always Rings Twice* with John Garfield, who was a good buddy of mine. One night I said to him, 'Julie'—his real name was Jules Garfinkel—'tell me the truth, you're bangin' Lana, aren't you?' 'No, Artie,' he says, 'I wouldn't touch her, she's your wife.' After a couple more drinks, I said to him, 'Come on, Julie, you can tell me. I know Lana, she needs the attention. And she's gorgeous, impossible to resist. I couldn't blame you.' Finally, a drink or two more, and Julie confesses. 'Okay, Artie,' he tells me, 'between scenes we take a ride and do it in the car.' So I divorced Lana, but Julie and I stayed friends until the day he died."

Artie was in psychotherapy for more than thirty years before he declared that it was bunk. He wrote books about it. He quit playing the clarinet and had his horn made into a lamp, which he showed to me, still working, in his living room. His compositions and recordings provided a comfortable income, and he taught music at colleges when he felt like it. Women continued to fascinate and interest him, but he stopped marrying them. His dislike for Benny Goodman—"as a person, not as a musician"—had not abated; Artie seemed happy to have outlived his nemesis.

We went together to a copy shop in a shopping mall crowded with teenagers. "Nobody in here ever heard of me," Artie said, "and neither have most of their parents.

It doesn't matter. I did some things. I had Lana next to me in the convertible. Now I have a novel to finish." I asked him what the novel was about. "Everything," he said, "only everything."

Lost Interlude

I remember going to see Jerry Lee Lewis perform at a roadhouse called the Rebel Room or the Rebel Rouser Room, I forget which, in Boonville, Missouri, in 1964, when I was eighteen. I was then attending the University of Missouri, which was just up the road, thirty miles away, in Columbia. I believe I went with my friend Tom Cooke, a locally prominent folk singer. Tom was a good songwriter, a pal of Arlo Guthrie's, and I thought he would be a big star, but by the late '60s he disappeared down the drug-filled rabbit hole of America. Too bad—Tom had a sweet voice, an easygoing, ingratiating style, he was handsome and a great guitar picker. I heard from his sister, Candy, sometime during the 1980s, who told me he had changed his name and had undergone a religious or lifestyle conversion of some kind. Tom wanted to tell me about it himself, she said, that he was going to write to me from Chicago, where he was living, but he never did and I don't know what became of him. But one winter night in 1964 we drove in Tom's '57 Chevy Bel-Air convertible to Boonville, Missouri, to witness the then professionally ostracized and publicly disgraced (for marrying his thirteen-year-old cousin, Myra) Jerry Lee Lewis shake down that redneck roadhouse. The Killer tore it up, too. I remember him saying to the 250 or so beer-guzzling louts in attendance (including Cooke and myself), "Man, for a while there, I was bigger'n Elvis." Then he ripped into "Little Queenie."

I'm writing this at six o'clock in the morning of October 31, 2003, in my hotel room in Graz, Austria, where I've come to attend the premiere of an opera based on the screenplay I wrote with David Lynch for a film he directed called *Lost Highway*. The opera, composed by Olga Neuwirth, with a libretto by Elfriede Jelinek, is also called *Lost Highway*. Before coming here, I stopped for a couple of days to see some friends in Zurich. Daniel Schmid, the Swiss film and opera director, with whom I recently wrote a screenplay for a movie called *Portovero*, and I went to visit our friend Beat Curti, who lives on a palatial estate next to Lake Zurich, which is located a few fortified doors down from Tina Turner's home. I told Beat that I'd seen Ike and Tina Turner perform at a dance in Columbia, Missouri, almost forty years before, around the same time I'd first seen Jerry Lee Lewis. Beat said that he and his wife, Regula, had gone with Tina and her husband to the south of France recently, to celebrate Tina's sixtieth birthday. Back when I saw her, Tina lived in St. Louis. She was an electrifying performer in those days, a stupefyingly exciting singer and dancer. I saw her and Ike again in a club in East St. Louis very early in 1965, in the company of Tom Cooke and a hillbilly singer from

Clarksville, Tennessee, named Jimmy James, who, like Cooke, shortly thereafter disappeared from my life. Beat Curti invited me back the next summer for an outdoor party at his new house to celebrate Daniel Schmid's and my movie. "We'll have a band," Beat said, "and I'll ask Tina to sing." That would be great, I told him. "Both Tina and I have come a long way from St. Louis, as the song says, in forty years." (Tina perhaps a little bit longer.)

Regarding this opera based on *Lost Highway*: Other than that the first few performances are scheduled to take place at the Steirischer Herbst music festival in Graz, followed by several more at the Theatre Basel in Switzerland, I don't know much. As I told Robert Hilferty, a cultural critic for the *New York Times*, when he called me to ask what I thought about the adaptation, I didn't even know the opera existed until the Steirischer Herbst company invited me to the premiere. I've often enjoyed operas, and I even wrote a libretto for one to be composed by Toru Takemitsu, at his request, for the Opéra de Lyon. (Takemitsu died before he wrote the music. The opera, entitled *Madrugada*, was subsequently composed by Toru-san's disciple, Ichiro Nodaira.) *Lost Highway*, the opera, is as yet a mystery to me—a feeling many viewers expressed about the film even after having seen it.

From Jerry Lee Lewis at the Rebel Room in Boonville, Missouri, to Ike and Tina Turner in East St. Louis, to Olga Neuwirth's musical interpretation of Lynch's and my version of what I only half-jokingly once referred to as "Orpheus and Eurydice Meet *Double Indemnity*," it's been, as the Grateful Dead described their own sojourn, a long, strange trip; a curious, unforgettable musical voyage I'm happy to have sailed.

It's now November 2, the morning after the morning after having attended the premiere performance of the opera. Olga Neuwirth's music is entirely appropriate to the play, conveying the necessary tension and overall feeling of uncertainty, desire, and dread. I got a kick out of the musicians' whistling and hissing; also the use of harmonica and accordion. The sets are interesting, consisting of moving walls, sliding pallets upon which prone performers are transported, and indistinct video images projected at crucial intervals. (Olga later told me that her original intention was to have only video, no live performance at all, but that Steirischer Herbst would not condone it.) The libretto is an abridged version of the original screenplay, with no new material added and no surprises.

The action follows the film almost too faithfully. Approximately one-third of the way into the ninety-minute opera, the performers begin to sing some of the dialogue. In the movie, there is a definite demarcation after the first forty-five minutes of the two-hour-and-nine-minute running length; and, unlike in Lynch's 1990 film adaptation of my novel *Wild at Heart*, nobody sings. The audience response at the conclusion of the opera was enthusiastic. On opening night, it's always difficult to know what that portends, owing to the fact that the house is usually packed with relatives, well-wishers, and sponsors. So-called avant-garde opera, or "new" music, seems to my inexpert ears and eyes as institutionalized as the more traditional or classical forms. Everyone—even most of the attendees—wears black; the sounds are dissonant, atonal, meant to disturb rather than soothe; the actor/singers appear out of joint, off-kilter, their movements fractured, attitudes desperate. Am I alone in this perception? One thing Toru Takemitsu, who was renowned for being a pioneer of new music, told me when we were working together on the libretto for *Madrugada*: "Must have beautiful duet!" In this operatic take on *Lost Highway*, I would have enjoyed hearing a beautiful duet, if just to interrupt for a moment the severity of it all. (Perhaps bedeviled Fred Madison and his alter id, the Mystery Man, combining symbiotically as the Kafka Twins!) As Ed or Lou, one of the detectives in the play, might say, "There's nothing wrong with a good interlude."

In the late 1960s or early '70s, Jerry Lee Lewis starred in a brief run of a musical version of *Othello* called *Catch My Soul*, the title being a phrase plucked from a line in Shakespeare's play. I never caught the show, which, I believe, was staged only in Los Angeles or New York. I think that he and Tina Turner would have been terrific in the opera of *Lost Highway* portraying Fred/Pete and Renee/Alice. I would have paid good money just to have heard their duet.

Madrugada
Not Opera—Action Musical!

In November 1993, I flew from Rome to Vienna to meet with the Japanese composer Toru Takemitsu; the Swiss film and opera director Daniel Schmid; the American conductor (and San Francisco resident) Kent Nagano; and Kent's co-artistic director at the Opéra de Lyon, Jean-Pierre Brossmann, to discuss the possibility of creating an original opera based on an idea of Takemitsu's. Later, we were joined by the conductor Seiji Ozawa, who was interested in staging the opera in Japan.

Nagano had asked Takemitsu in 1987 to come up with an idea for an opera. For more than five years, Kent told me, Toru had fruitlessly searched for the right librettist. When he suggested that I might be the person to do it, Kent and Schmid agreed immediately, and together the three of them called me from the Hotel Kempinski in Berlin, where they were staying, and invited me to meet them in Vienna, where a retrospective of Takemitsu's music was being performed at the opera house.

Toru had by this time in his forty-year career composed ninety film scores, for directors such as Kurosawa

(*Ran, Do'des ka-den, Kagemusha*), Teshiga-hara (*Woman in the Dunes*), and Philip Kaufman (*Rising Sun*); and produced classical pieces that had earned him virtually every major award in the field. He had invited me to write the libretto based on his admiration, he said, for my novel *Wild at Heart*, which had recently gained an international following and been adapted for a film that won the prestigious Palme d'Or at the Cannes Film Festival; and for my poetry, which Takemitsu felt reflected a sensibility that had much in common with the Chinese and Japanese poets, who had influenced his own work.

As Takemitsu spoke at our first meeting, describing his dream, his vision, in his halting, elliptical English, I was charmed by his childlike, expressive face and elegant hand gestures. Toru was a small, fragile-looking man, but his inner strength was obvious: he had the fierce heart of a poet, which he also was. I liked him immediately, and we agreed to collaborate on the project. I began outlining the libretto on the seventh of February 1994.

That first meeting, at the Imperial Palace Hotel—the former residence of Emperor Franz Joseph—in Vienna, the birthplace of my father, proved to be a memorable one. Also staying at our hotel was Mikhail Gorbachev's right-hand man, whose name I forget, who had come to Austria to ask President Kurt Waldheim for money. Austrian soldiers, armed with automatic weapons, stood guard on the Ringstrasse in front of the Imperial Palace, and the hallways of the hotel were patrolled by members of the KGB. I felt as if we were minor characters in a

Graham Greene novel. One evening, we were introduced to the mayor of Vienna, who had come to the hotel to meet with Gorbachev's emissary; a week later, the mayor—whose visit was a matter of some controversy—lost several of his fingers while opening a package addressed to him that contained a bomb.

I met with Takemitsu twice more: in San Francisco in January 1994, and in Tokyo in September of that year. He guided me through the composition of the libretto—I'd never written one before—and by the spring of 1995, it was virtually completed. I titled the opera *Madrugada*, a Spanish word meaning the time just before dawn, which was intended as a metaphor. Toru was very excited to begin writing the music, he told me, but that spring he fell ill and had to be hospitalized. He was soon diagnosed with cancer, and, due to his rapidly deteriorating condition, Takemitsu's composition did not progress beyond the most preliminary stage. Despite his epistolary assurances to me that he would recover, he did not. Toru, who had become my dear friend, died on February 20, 1996, before he could see his dream realized.

Takemitsu sent me several notes from his hospital bed. Among my favorites were: "*Madrugada* is not opera, action musical"; and "Must have beautiful duet!" The futuristic story is about a young girl named Yumi who rebels against a society in which all memories have been banned and possession of photographs is a criminal offense. She is a Joan of Arc–like heroine (minus the madness) who, with the help of cetaceans, saves the mostly frightened, trembling world from a fate worse than fascism. Toru, whose only child was a daughter, Maki, wrote touchingly to me: "I have one proposal for a small revision. I have some doubts on the scene in The Dreams (Part One) where Yumi quarrels with her parents. I expect Yumi being very delicate, sensitive and full of dreams, with sympathy for people. Such a girl should behave even when she quarrels with parents, I expect ... [At] present here conversation with parents sounds too punky for me. She should not be a baby gangstar [sic] of the West Coast." Accordingly, I did my best to follow Toru's directive.

It was several years before Kent Nagano called me to say that *Madrugada* would be completed, after all. Ichiro Nodaira, a disciple of Takemitsu's who had recorded Toru's piano music and was an esteemed composer in his own right, had agreed to take on the task of writing the opera, which would be a unique experience for him, as well. I met with Ichiro and Kent in San Francisco in 2002, after which Ichiro began to compose the score, completing it in the spring of 2005.

When Nagano informed me that, due to his efforts, *Madrugada* would premiere at the Schleswig-Holstein Musik Festival in Kiel, Germany, in August of the same year, my first thought was of Toru, that his dream had been kept alive. I recalled what Takemitsu had written in an essay in 1971: "Too often these days creativity is nothing but the invention of methods. When aesthetics become so sharp and distinguished, art becomes weak." I hoped that Nagano, Nodaira, and I would not disappoint Takemitsu, wherever he would be listening.

The preceding was written literally in the time before dawn, on an airplane in flight from San Francisco to Frankfurt, Germany, five days prior to the premiere of *Madrugada* at the opera house in Kiel. My first night there, I was taken to a rehearsal of the singers, where I was reunited with Nagano and Nodaira. They told me that the vocalists were excited by the quirkiness and unconventional language of the libretto. David Coleman, Kent's assistant, agreed. "None of them," he said, "has previously had the opportunity, in this form, to express emotions so colloquially." I wasn't certain at the time that he meant this as a compliment, but he smiled when he said it. "The words won't matter," I replied, "if the music is good." This is what I had told Takemitsu in Tokyo the last time I saw him.

At the press conference two days before the premiere, I repeated what I'd said to Takemitsu and Coleman, and everyone laughed, including the other participants: Nodaira and Nagano; Peter Schmidt, the director and set designer; and Rolf Beck, president of the Schleswig-Holstein Musik Festival. They may all have thought that I was joking, but I was serious. Half of the time it's next to impossible to understand what the singers are saying anyway; if the music is sublime, one can always close one's eyes, forget about the actors/singers, and just listen.

I was impressed at the second day of rehearsals by the sixty-piece orchestra, comprised of musicians from twenty-two countries. The principal singers were a geographically eclectic group, as well, having come from England, Germany, Korea, Russia, and elsewhere. Nodaira's music was by turns atonal and melodic, making me think of it as Elmer Bernstein meets Takemitsu, with the flavor of Messiaen, with whom Nodaira studied in France. At times, it reminded me of Bernstein's jazzy score for the film *The Man with the Golden Arm* (the first record album I ever bought), with echoes of Shelley Manne on drums, Shorty Rogers on fluegelhorn, and the Candoli brothers, Pete and Conte, on trumpets. Suddenly, there came a mood swing that put me in mind of rainy city streets at night, shadowy shapes disappearing down dark alleys; the stuff of film noir. Then came lightning cracks, followed by shudders and moans, before the unearthly but hauntingly beautiful intercession of the counter tenor. Anything and everything goes, I thought, which was consistent with the original concept. I had told Toru that I intended to make his opera a multi-formed event, utilizing film and special effects to illustrate the text and music. He approved of this approach and encouraged me to "throw in sink kitchen."

Opening night. *Madrugada* will be performed twice at the festival. It is being recorded and filmed by German radio and television. Takemitsu's widow and daughter have flown in from Japan to attend the premiere; I realize that I have not seen them for ten years. It's been eighteen years since Kent Nagano first asked Toru to write an opera. It's a momentous occasion most of all, however, for Ichiro Nodaira, whose first opera this is.

At the dress rehearsal, I saw that many of the things I had written into the libretto, such as the use of video, film, and a number of special effects, had not been integrated as intended; and so I suggested to Kent Nagano, as the chief of production, that they be scrapped and the staging simplified in order to better showcase the music. The manner in which Peter Schmidt had implemented these ideas, as far as I was concerned, amounted to superfluous kitsch that served only to distract the audience. The characters who came off best were Lágrimas, the Vampira/Gagool philosopher-witch, and the harlequin-like hermaphrodite Azul, who comments on the action throughout, speaking directly to the audience, and who has the last word. I was very interested to see how seriously these and other suggestions of mine, such as changing the costume of the main character, Yumi, to better reflect her personality, were taken.

After the performance: big relief. Virtually all of my post–dress rehearsal suggestions were adopted, and the performances, to my imperfect ear, seemed close to flawless. The audience response was overwhelming. Most important, none of the 750 attendees walked out during the one hour and thirty-five minutes of running time; and, at the conclusion, Nagano, Nodaira, Schmidt, and I, along with the principal cast members, participated in repeated curtain calls. During one of the last of these, Kent said to me, "This is amazing. I can't really remember ever having been called back for so many bows."

Takemitsu's idea for an "action musical," on this night, anyway, seemed to be a success. Toru's widow and daughter were pleased, and the two leading music critics from Tokyo, who attended with them, were effusive in their praise of what one of them told me was "the first original modern Japanese opera." I didn't fall asleep, of course, until *madrugada*.

MADRUGADA
The Libretto

―――――

Libretto by Barry Gifford
Story by Barry Gifford, Daniel Schmid,
and Toru Takemitsu

Based on an idea by Toru Takemitsu

Dedicated to:
TORU TAKEMITSU
8 October 1930–20 February 1996

and to Asaka
and Maki

"What a wonderful sweet man Toru-san was and if there's any consolation (there isn't actually) then, that we were so fortunate to have met such a person. The Japanese people here were all crying yesterday late at night and we did a kind of a 'wake'—wishing Toru-san a good journey, wherever he's going."

—Daniel Schmid, in a letter to Barry Gifford from the Hotel Savoy, Berlin, 21 February 1996

"[T]he verses which the librettist writes are not addressed to the public but are really a private letter to the composer."

—W. H. Auden

"Too often these days creativity is nothing but the invention of methods. When aesthetics become so sharp and distinguished, art becomes weak."

—Toru Takemitsu, 1971

Madrugada

ma·dru·ga·da *f.* Spanish (*amanecer*) dawn; (*levantada*) early rising *de m.* at daybreak, very early; the time before the dawn

Cast

YUMI . . . . .a seventeen-year-old girl/woman

TEVA . . . . .a young man about Yumi's age

VERA. . . . . .her mother

ROJO . . . . .her father

AZUL . . . . the hermaphrodite (appears alternately as male or female of indeterminate age, an outlaw)

POLICEMEN

LÁGRIMAS . . . . an old woman

PRISON GUARDS / OFFICIALS

SOLDIERS

INTRO:

The Veil of Illusion

THE PLAY:

The Dreams (Part One)
The Dreams (Part Two)
The Dialogues (Part One)
The Table Manners of Cannibals (Part One)
The Dreams (Part Three)
The Table Manners of Cannibals (Part Two)
The Dialogues (Part Two)
The Dreams (Part Four)
The Dialogues (Part Three)
The Table Manners of Cannibals (Parts Three)
The Table Manners of Cannibals (Part Four)
The Dialogues (Part Four)
The Dreams (Part Five)
Madrugada

CODA:

The Memory of Love

INTRO—The Veil of Illusion

Instead of rising or parting, the "curtain" begins *burning* from the bottom toward the top. As the flames rise, the curtain burns unevenly, shredding, causing gaps in the fabric, large rends and tears that allow the audience to glimpse through the crumbling facade. What they see are pure horror scenes: Bosch-like landscapes, figures writhing in pain and agony, attacking and killing each other; going up in flames themselves; horrible, unimaginable creatures only half-glimpsed, so that the viewer cannot really be certain of what he has seen; buildings, skyscrapers crashing to the ground as in an earthquake or as if having been bombed; monstrous apparitions pass in the distance; lightning, wind, and firestorms followed by hail and blinding rain. The curtain—the *veil* of illusion—is finally torn to bits, burned, disappeared. The stage goes BLACK and SILENT.

The Dreams (Part One)

The BEACH AT NIGHT. A YOUNG WOMAN is sleeping on the beach. The sky is black.

A monumental TRAFFIC JAM. Cars are stretched bumper to bumper across the stage and into the background as far as the eye can see. People are hollering, angry, blaring their horns. They get out of their cars to argue with one another. Fistfights break out, women and men alike. One man pulls a gun and shoots another driver. A woman stabs the gunman in the back. Police arrive. There is CHAOS as the prisoners of this terminal traffic jam riot. They are out of control and their fury and panic cannot be contained by the police.

FADE TO BLACK

Across the dimly lit stage run a dozen or more CHICKENS WITHOUT HEADS.

Just before dawn. The YOUNG WOMAN lies sleeping on the beach. As the light intensifies, she stirs and sits up, watching the colors come alive over the water. Finally, she rises and walks offstage.

The YOUNG WOMAN enters a house through a back door, into the kitchen. She opens the refrigerator door and takes out a bottle of juice, opens it, pours some into a glass and drinks it.

An OLDER WOMAN, the young woman's mother, enters the kitchen. They stare at each other before speaking.

MOTHER
Yumi! You just gettin' in, ain't you? Where you been all night? Who you been with?

YUMI
Nobody. I was by myself.

MOTHER
You're just a tramp. Always goin' off at night, not tellin' nobody nothin.' All the time I gotta lie to your daddy, cover your ass.

YUMI
I ain't askin' you to protect me from him. I'll be all right.

MOTHER
Your daddy been through the back door of hell for us!

YUMI'S FATHER enters.

FATHER
What's goin' on in here? Where you been, Yumi?

YUMI
Listening.

FATHER
Listening? Listening to what?

VERA
Leave her be, Rojo. She's tired.

ROJO
Hellfire, woman, we got any coffee?

VERA
I'll make some, Rojo. Go lie down and I'll call you when it's ready.

ROJO leaves.

YUMI

Mama, I . . . I can't stay here no more.

VERA (making coffee)

You do what you want, then. You're seventeen years old, I won't stop you.

YUMI goes for the door. Stops.

YUMI

There's things I know about, Mama. Things that happened in the time before, maybe. I hear about 'em.

VERA

Stop talkin' trash, Yumi. Ain't nothin' worth knowin' about the time before. You know the law. *What's past is past.* Only thing matters is now. Anybody caught talkin' about the time before is banished to the sea, you know that. And drownin' ain't a pretty way to die.

Suddenly, YUMI turns to her mother, and speaks tenderly.

YUMI

I'm goin,' Mama. Good-bye.

VERA

You ain't here today, you'll be gone tomorrow, too.

YUMI, in a sudden display of affection, embraces her mother. VERA, reluctant at first, hugs back. YUMI leaves.

End of The Dreams (Part One)

The Dreams (Part Two)

A nightclub. CUSTOMERS are gathered at the tables, drinking, talking, laughing. Occasionally (perhaps) a fight breaks out, which is quickly broken up by the waiters, bouncers, or other customers. The music is loud, raucous jazz. Suddenly a WOMAN and a MAN appear on a stage in the nightclub. They stalk each other in a kind of sensuous circling dance. (The music accompanies their movements.) As the dance continues, they gradually shed their clothes and simulate copulation. The customers mostly ignore them.

We hear the whir of a projector and a film flashes onto a giant screen: it's *KING KONG*, the scene in Kong's lair on Skull Mountain, where he has brought the girl. Kong is attacked by a snake-monster and they fight until the mighty Kong crushes the reptile to death, then stands out on his mountain balcony and beats his chest and roars as the captive woman recoils, terrified.

Next on screen comes the scene from *Frankenstein* where the little girl is gathering flowers and is confronted by the monster. She hands him a flower, which he delicately takes into his own giant hand.

The next scene is from Cocteau's *Beauty and the Beast*, when Beauty is suddenly confronted by the Beast.

Next comes Murnau's *Nosferatu*, the vampire rising from Mina's bed, panicked by the rising sun.

Finally, a clip from *The Beast from 20,000 Fathoms*, when the sea creature rises during the night and devours a Japanese ship and all of its crew.

YUMI, who has again been asleep on the beach, is startled awake by this final image. She rises and walks into a city resembling Tangier, Algiers, or Marrakech, a coastal city of Arab or African origin—white, red-brown, blue. People pass as if she, or they, are invisible. YUMI negotiates the twisting, caracole-like streets of this place out of time, an indefinable, unidentifiable city.

She enters a dimly lit cafeteria, a long room out of an Edward Hopper painting of the New York of the 1930s. Single men and women are seated, apart from one another, not speaking, heads bent over a cup of coffee or bowl of soup. They are lonely, shabby images. YUMI seems lost as she surveys the room. Nobody raises their eyes to look at her. She sees someone she knows and runs to him, a YOUNG MAN her own age.

YUMI

Teva! What're you doin' here? It's good to see you, I need to talk to someone.

TEVA

Oh, hey, Yumi! Where've you been hidin'?

YUMI

Haven't been, really. I got kicked out of my house, or maybe I just left.

TEVA

Don't matter, does it? Where you gonna go?

YUMI

I been sleepin' on the beach, a place where I've been hangin' out, anyway. Some spooky things been happenin' to me there, Teva. You ought to come.

TEVA

What do you mean, spooky?

YUMI

I see stuff, mostly while I'm asleep. And sometimes I hear people talkin' all kinds of noise I don't understand. I got a notion it's all about the time before.

TEVA

Dreams, Yumi. Them are dreams you're havin'. You're supposed to forget 'em.

YUMI

Hell, Teva, I know what dreams are, even if it is against the law to admit to havin' 'em. This is another thing altogether. I can't figure out what to make of it. They're what I guess are called visions, though

I ain't sure, since I don't know nobody who's had one. Come on, Teva, come with me. Maybe you'll be able to explain it.

TEVA
Okay, Yumi, long as nobody finds out what we're doin.'

YUMI
Why should they? Nobody's ever paid attention to what I've said or done up to now.

End of The Dreams (Part Two)

The Dialogues (Part One)

The beach at dusk. YUMI and TEVA sit together and watch the sun disappear into the ocean.

> TEVA
>
> It ain't that I don't want to know about the time before, just it never seemed important.

> YUMI
>
> I wasn't lookin' to hear or see anything—it's like I been chosen.

> TEVA
>
> Chosen? Who by?

> YUMI
>
> I don't have no ready answers, Teva. I think you just have to see for yourself. Wait with me tonight and maybe it'll come clear.

The waves lap at the shore. As the VOICES are heard, we see the characters and events described.

VOICE #1

The earth shudders
When I hear
Your voice
My eyes lower
When we meet
Is there no way
To prevent
Your capturing
My heart?

VOICE #2

With the rains
I ceased my travels
Holed up in
A mountain hut
I wrote love letters
To a distant friend
Knowing
That when I left
I would
Leave them behind.

VOICE #3

You kept our secret
Through these years
Now I am free
And you are gone

No surprise
Of all feelings
It's sadness
That endures.

VOICE #1

This summer
More than before
Storms miss land
Each morning
Fresh flowers
In the green
Peacock vase.

VOICE #2

Cranes slowly
settle on
nearby pond
Clouds blow though
no lovers
or friends
Birds, weather
Will do.

VOICE #3

On an island
Surrounded by swans
One after another

Lands nearby
None more invisible
Than I.

Faint light appears again on the horizon. YUMI and TEVA stir. They sit up and stare at each other.

End of The Dialogues (Part One)

The Table Manners of Cannibals (Part One)

YUMI is onstage in a concert hall, the lead singer for a rock band. TEVA is playing guitar among the other musicians behind her. The hall is filled with young people who gradually respond to the band's music.

                YUMI (sings)

VERSE
- Everything they tell you is lies
- Can't even look in your eyes
- But it's not you they despise
- Just try this on for size

CHORUS
- What do you know
- About the time before?
- Don't you think it's time
- That we explore
- What's in the past?
- And do it fast!

	I know your life ain't nice
VERSE	No time to tell you this twice
	The language can't be precise
	With your head caught in a vise
	What do you know
	About the time before?

REPEAT	Don't you think it's time
CHORUS	That we explore
	What's in the past?
	And do it fast!

As YUMI and the band perform, thrashing around on the stage, police enter the concert hall and begin an attempt to contain the excitement of the audience. Their repressive tactics have the opposite effect, however, and soon, with the band increasing their intensity, the scene turns savage, with police and spectators fighting.

YUMI (sings)

	They say what's in the past is past
VERSE	But you know that can't last
	One generation was gassed
	Another wiped out by a blast

What do you know
About the time before?

REPEAT	Don't you think it's time
CHORUS	That we explore
	What's in the past?
	And do it fast!

The riot continues. More police arrive and destroy the band's instruments, dragging the musicians off the stage. YUMI and TEVA break away and run together out of the concert hall as chaos reigns.

End of The Table Manners of Cannibals (Part One)

The Dreams (Part Three)

Thunder and lightning. Lightning strikes a giant tree on the stage, splitting it in two. From the wound in the tree rises a fantastic, naked HERMAPHRODITE whose hair, like Medusa's, is a tangle of writhing serpents. The HERMAPHRODITE steps away from the sizzling, cloven tree trunk and dances provocatively while speaking.

> HERMAPHRODITE
> There was a time before loneliness, a time nobody remembers, when the earth's revolutions revealed desire and the exquisite pain of love. Fear is all that's left, disguised as peace.

Projected on a screen behind the HERMAPHRODITE are these scenes:

—Old people seated on benches in a park, scattering bread crumbs to pigeons.
—Close-ups of women kissing women.
—Close-ups of men kissing men.

—Close-ups of men and women kissing.

—Close-ups of animals having sex.

—Repeat clip of old people seated on benches in a park tossing bread crumbs to pigeons and repeat all film clips in sequence.

HERMAPHRODITE

Life is only a phase we're going through. Don't worry, take your time. It's so confusing. There's never enough food. There's never enough money. There's never enough of whatever it is you might think you need. Think beyond need. Who says you don't know what you're doing? Who knows what you're doing? Do you? Do you know what's being done? Who do you know who has time to do it? Can you do it? Time is out. Time is money. There's money in food. In time you'll know. Who knows time? If you stop to kiss my ass I'll give you the time of day. You don't need to listen to this. You can run. Keep running. All there is to run out of is time. Keep time. Keep it to yourself. It's all you know.

YUMI and TEVA are shivering on the beach. The sky is in turmoil, a cold wind is blowing.

YUMI

Do you believe me now?

> TEVA
>
> I believe in you.

> YUMI
>
> I'm frightened, just like everybody else.

> TEVA
>
> You've got a funny way of not showing it.

> YUMI
>
> We can't give up now. There's no place for us, Teva, unless we make it.

YUMI and TEVA draw closer together. They look up. The sky becomes even more spectacular, a panorama of violent colors culminating in a shower of stars that engulf YUMI and TEVA, covering them completely as they speak.

> YUMI (to the sky)
>
> How is it possible to no longer be responsible for one who has given you his heart?

> YUMI and TEVA
>
> The magic that works within us
> is time passing—
> We have no guidance, no way
> to know what will come.
> Because of this we are desperate

and want so much to hold,
to bury ourselves in others,
and sit, briefly flickering,
like candles, waiting for the wind.

End of The Dreams (Part Three)

The Table Manners of Cannibals (Part Two)

YUMI'S PARENTS' HOUSE. The middle of the night. ROJO and VERA are sleeping in their beds when the POLICE break in, knocking over lamps and chairs, storming the place. Police torches provide the only light.

POLICEMAN #1
We know she's hiding here! Give her up! The boy, too!

VERA and ROJO sit up in bed as the POLICE crash into the bedroom.

POLICEMAN #2
We want Yumi! And the boy, Teva! Where are they?

VERA
They ain't here! I swear, they ain't!

ROJO

We ain't seen 'em. Yumi left off livin' with us a while ago.

POLICEMAN #1

Search all the rooms! Look under the rugs, make sure there's no trapdoors. Check the roof!

POLICEMAN #2 (to VERA and ROJO)

Get dressed, you're coming with us.

ROJO

What for? Yumi's not here, hasn't been here. We told you.

VERA

We don't know where she is!

POLICEMAN #1

Drag 'em out of here if they won't cooperate.

ROJO (getting up)

No, no, we're comin.'

VERA (getting dressed)

We'll cooperate! We'll cooperate!

POLICEMAN #3

Look at these!

POLICEMAN #2

Photographs!

POLICEMAN #3

I found 'em in the girl's room.

ROJO

Photographs! Vera, you know about this?

VERA

Yumi said she'd destroyed them! I told her to get rid of 'em!

POLICEMAN #1

You know the law against taking or possessing photographs or film.

ROJO

What's past is past! We know! Those aren't ours, they're hers!

VERA

Not ours! Yumi's!

POLICEMAN #2

Simple possession of a single photograph carries an automatic, unpardonable prison sentence of thirteen years. How many have you found?

POLICEMAN #3
There must be a dozen, more.

POLICEMAN #2
Two lifetimes' worth.

POLICEMAN #1
Unless you give her up! Tell us where she is—and the boy—it could make a difference.

ROJO
Yes, yes! We'll tell you.

VERA
Rojo! You know?

ROJO
I think they ... they must be ... maybe they're ...

POLICEMAN #1
Take 'em away.

ROJO
No! We didn't ... we ...

VERA
We follow the rules! We've forgotten the time before! No time! No time!

OTHER POLICEMEN drag VERA and ROJO out of the house. POLICEMAN #1 and #2 remain inside, studying the photographs by flashlight.

> POLICEMAN #1
>
> Pretty amazing stuff.

> POLICEMAN #2
>
> Any we should keep for ourselves?

> POLICEMAN #1
>
> Look at this one.

> POLICEMAN #2
>
> Sunset. At the beach. What else?

> POLICEMAN #1
>
> Faces. All kinds of faces.

> POLICEMAN #2
>
> This is serious. How do you suppose she got this way?

> POLICEMAN #1
>
> Who, the girl?

> POLICEMAN #2
>
> Yeah. I don't think her parents are responsible. They don't seem the type.

POLICEMAN #1
They seldom do. But you're right. These people kept clean.

POLICEMAN #2
The mother knew about these, though. The photographs.

POLICEMAN #1
Here, you keep the sunset. I'll take one of a flight of birds.

POLICEMAN #2
We can get plenty for a few of these and still have enough to put 'em away forever.

POLICEMAN #1
Won't hurt us any when the promotions are handed out.

They both laugh at their seeming good fortune and EXIT the house.

End of The Table Manners of Cannibals (Part Two)

The Dialogues (Part Two)

YUMI and TEVA are running. They stop, exhausted. A figure approaches, indistinct in a fog. YUMI and TEVA are frightened, but too fatigued to run. They prepare for a fight until they see that the person coming closer is an OLD WOMAN.

TEVA

Who are you?

OLD WOMAN

Lágrimas. Call me Lágrimas.

YUMI

Do you know us, Lágrimas? We might not be folks you should be seen with.

LÁGRIMAS

No one has seen me for decades. If you live for as long as I have, people will pretend not to see you, too.

TEVA

Why is that?

LÁGRIMAS

It's easier for them, of course. The particularities of life overwhelmed most of the population. The pressure became too much for them and the result . . . well, you live with the result.

YUMI

Or you die.

LÁGRIMAS

Or withdraw, as I did.

YUMI

Has that helped?

LÁGRIMAS

I suppose it's satisfactory. But beauty strengthens me. It's kept me alive.

TEVA

Beauty?

LÁGRIMAS

Yes, I'll tell you. But you're cold and tired. Come with me.

YUMI and TEVA follow LÁGRIMAS to her shelter, a hut not very far from the beach. They sit near a fire and LÁGRIMAS gives them something warm to drink.

YUMI
This is where you live?

LÁGRIMAS
I'm never bothered here. As I told you, most people don't really see me. I'm better off being invisible.

TEVA
Yes! On the beach, we heard about this—being invisible! Yumi, do you remember?

YUMI
Yeah, I remember. Now we can both remember.

LÁGRIMAS
Here are a few small stories you may wish to remember:
Back at my hut nobody bothers me
Flies buzz around my head
I lie beside yellow flowers
And watch the fog blow away

Worst things that can happen:
Get bit by bugs, get poked

By pine needles or blackberry thorns
Squatting outside at night

On my door I've tacked a painting
Entitled "Door to the River"—inside's nothing much
Axe, books, broom, a container of water
Never more than three days old

Fleas are my worst enemy
I give my money away
I never thought this would happen
To me
I call this place "Snail Hut" like Chao-Hsien's
Because it's so small, or "Honeysuckle Hut"
Because of vines overhanging the entrance
Late at night I stand dreaming in my perfumed doorway.
A friend once told me
To truly understand what's inside my heart
I must keep apart, remind myself
It's not necessary to be smart

If often I appear righteous
It's only that
I'm still too fond
Of the world
Ate, watered plants

Walked to creek
Napped in orchard
Dreaming of my children

YUMI and TEVA have dropped their cups and fallen asleep. LÁGRIMAS tends to the fire.

End of The Dialogues (Part Two)

The Dreams (Part Four)

While YUMI and TEVA sleep, LÁGRIMAS stokes the fire and the smoke drifts above their heads, spreading out across the stage, enveloping it in a mist. The mist clears, and via a sequence of projected photographs and films—and perhaps live enactments—we see a variety of images.

Note: Images to come, suggesting those things that human beings should never have done or become involved with in the first place.

The smoky mist from the fire rises again and covers the stage.

End of The Dreams (Part Four)

Dialogues (Part Three)

LÁGRIMAS is leading YUMI and TEVA down a winding stone stairway into the bowels of an ancient church, much of which is in ruins. The old woman is carrying a torch, lighting the way.

                LÁGRIMAS
This edifice was once a church, a synagogue, a mosque where people came to communicate with their God. Only the Holy Ghost was listening, of course.

                    YUMI
This was a house of faith?

                LÁGRIMAS
Faith being the evidence of things not seen.

                    TEVA
What's down here, in this pit?

They come to a chamber filled with caskets, some open, most closed, decorated with paintings of skulls and crossbones and roses.

LÁGRIMAS

This was a burial ground for the wealthy. The rarefied atmosphere of the catacombs was believed to preserve the body indefinitely; and, as you can see, there are indeed a goodly number of leathery remains.

YUMI

But why?

LÁGRIMAS

In the hope that they might one day be resurrected, but it was the devil's game (extending her torchlight). You see the stacks of bones amongst the crypts? Further evidence of faith.

TEVA

What about the devil?

LÁGRIMAS

It was written that an angel descended from heaven with a chain and the key to the bottomless pit. The angel bound the Devil and cast him into the pit to endure a wait of one thousand years. The dead lived not again until the thousand years were finished.

Some say the Devil's sentence has expired, that he is loosed out of his prison and, now is the time of his resurrection.

YUMI

Do you believe this?

LÁGRIMAS

Devil is Lived spelled backwards. People fear the time before, what has been lived. This fear is expressed in many ways.

TEVA

What's past is past, that's the law.

LÁGRIMAS

The past is a river that flows through us. A river meanders, changes course. We change our ground or drown. But the source of the river remains the same.

LÁGRIMAS leads YUMI and TEVA back up the stairs out of the catacomb. As they disappear, the VOICES, embodied by spirits from the coffins, which we see, speak:

VOICE #1

After morning rain
Fine sprinkle
Blown from trees

VOICE #2

Lonely for conversation
The scholar in the mountain hut
Goes on reading

VOICE #3

Sign of rain:
The apple-less
Apple tree

VOICE #4

Across the
Snowy pasture
Two companions

VOICE #5

The fly on the leaf
Look again,
Only sun!

VOICE #6

Dead sea lion
Washed on shore
Flies buzz inside

VOICE #7

Late afternoon
Gathering firewood
In the rain

VOICE #8

The moon
Sits impaled
on the ears
of a rabbit—
Wild ducks soar
through a hole
in the purple air.

YUMI and TEVA are walking together on the beach. They each extend a hand to the other—they touch and embrace for the first time.

End of The Dialogues (Part Three)

The Table Manners of Cannibals (Part Three)

———

People are running through the streets, terrified, screaming. The POLICE are beating them, dragging citizens out of houses, ransacking homes and businesses. Over a loudspeaker on a truck or van rolling slowly through the center of this chaotic scene comes a TERRIBLE VOICE.

> TERRIBLE VOICE
> What's past is past! Today is the way!
> The time before exists no more!
> We are searching for the girl, Yumi,
> and the boy, Teva. Deliver them to us and
> peace will be restored. No citizen shall
> disturb the present! Today is the way!
> What's past is past, it cannot last!

YUMI'S PARENTS, ROJO and VERA, are visible on a giant television screen. They are shown in the same catacombs to which LÁGRIMAS has taken YUMI and TEVA. ROJO and VERA, overseen by guards with weapons, are going from coffin to coffin with torches, setting the corpses on fire.

From the midst of the madness loosed in the streets struts forward the HERMAPHRODITE, who blithely ignores all that is going on around and behind him/her.

                HERMAPHRODITE
Oh, you thought this was a dream?
You've seen it before?
Life's only what it seems,
Never more!
That sounds so familiar,
But never mind—
What's gone before
Is such a bore;
Besides, *they'll* treat you so unkind!
But here now, listen,
I'm just waiting—
In fact, I'm actually salivating—
The day will come
When freaks like me
Are proof of some
Sort of spirituality!

(Explosions are heard, sirens, helicopters, etc.)

            HERMAPHRODITE (cont'd.)
Shit! A freak can't even think in this place! If I step out of rhyme, I'm out of time, so I'll be brief. Listen: Happiness is a trick. Love is a trick. These are the only two tricks you can eat off forever. And *lest*

you forget, a man or a woman—as such the case may be—has got to eat!

(Even more explosions, wailing sirens, airplane noises, indistinct announcements.)

> HERMAPHRODITE
> This is too much for me. It's terrible, isn't it, the way manners have deteriorated, or just disappeared altogether? The absence of manners destroys civilized society—destroys the possibility of a civilized society. But you all know this already, or you wouldn't be at a goddamned *opera*!

The HERMAPHRODITE disappears into the background and the lights and *sounds grow dim, dimmer, dimmest.*

In the faint light we see LÁGRIMAS, trailed by YUMI and TEVA, sneaking across the stage. LÁGRIMAS continues offstage, but YUMI and TEVA linger to kiss and embrace.

Out of the darkness the POLICE appear, wielding guns and flashlights. A spotlight lands on YUMI and TEVA, who are seized forcibly by the POLICE. The couple are dragged off in custody.

The HERMAPHRODITE steps forward, into the spotlight.

HERMAPHRODITE (sings)

O fly
Wouldst I
the size
Of thee,
Or bee,
O yes, yes
one of those
to sleep
for ever
in a rose

FADE TO BLACK.

End of The Table Manners of Cannibals (Part Three)

The Table Manners of Cannibals (Part Four)

―――

YUMI and TEVA are in adjoining cells. A PRISON GUARD enters the cellblock and goes up to YUMI'S cell.

GUARD
You've got some visitors coming. Stand close to the bars and hold onto them.

TEVA
Yumi! What's goin' on?

GUARD (to TEVA)
Take it easy, kid! You'll get yours soon enough!

YUMI
Who's here?

YUMI'S PARENTS, ROJO and VERA, both manacled, enter the cellblock accompanied by several more GUARDS. They march to YUMI'S cell and halt in front of her.

> GUARD #2

Is this your daughter?

> ROJO and VERA

Yes, she is.

> GUARD #2

In your view, has she violated laws of the state?

> ROJO and VERA

Yes, she has.

> GUARD #2

She has possessed photographs, books, and other forbidden materials?

> ROJO and VERA

Yes, she has.

> GUARD #2

She has spread false information and conspired to incite riots, thereby fomenting behavior injurious to the state?

> ROJO and VERA

Yes, she has.

GUARD #2

Do you hereby publicly and formally renounce your parental responsibility for the girl, Yumi, and disassociate yourselves from her in every way?

ROJO and VERA

Yes, we do.

GUARD #2

(to other GUARDS) Take them away.
(to YUMI) You, Yumi, are to be banished by being set adrift on the ocean on a raft without provisions. This sentence shall be carried out before the next dawn.

GUARD #2 (cont'd.)

(to TEVA) You, Teva, are to be imprisoned for ten years in preparation for reeducation by the state.

The GUARDS EXIT the cellblock.

TEVA

Yumi, what can we do? We can't let 'em do this to you!

YUMI

Something'll happen. Remember what Lágrimas said about faith bein' the evidence of things not seen. We gotta have faith there's somethin' comin' we never could imagine.

End of The Table Manners of Cannibals (Part Four)

The Dialogues (Part Four)

LÁGRIMAS is at the beach. She walks to the ocean's edge and gestures at the water.

LÁGRIMAS

I am no painter
but when
a red bird
bursts from
green pine
into a grey
rain sky
it leaves itself
a part
of my
eye

VOICE #1

Past midnight in the cell
She is sad, sad
Such a short distance
From here

VOICE #2

Dreaming she's an eagle
Gliding hills filled
With snow, watching
Horses stumbling below

VOICE #3

Sitting still, lilacs,
Honeysuckle, occasional cats
Toughening mind like escaping
Past lives—highly unlikely

LÁGRIMAS

So often full of bitterness
I don't want to be
But nothing else can make me speak
It truly is the heart I seek

End of The Dialogues (Part Four)

The Dreams (Part Five)

―――――

YUMI is in her prison cell, staring out a small blue window a few hours before her banishment and seemingly certain death. The HERMAPHRODITE appears in YUMI'S cell, and with a gesture causes her to fall asleep. The HERMAPHRODITE now turns to the audience and puts a finger to his/her lips, the signal for silence. He/she then lies down next to YUMI and covers her with his/her arms.

Now begins a parade of PHANTOM SOLDIERS. They march through YUMI'S cell as she sleeps:

GHOSTLIKE SOLDIERS IN UNIFORM, depicting war fodder of the centuries, stream in single file (perhaps in two directions), a seemingly endless line in military regalia dating from before the Roman Empire to the present day. All so-called civilizations, cultures, tribes, should be represented here, carrying weapons: Zulus bearing shields and spears; Oglala Sioux; samurai; Prussian infantry; British redcoats; Vietcong clad in black pajamas; Japanese Zero pilots; minions of Alexander the Great,

Napoleon, Hitler; French Zouaves; every army in the history of mankind arrayed in an unprecedented pantheon of warriors.

As they march, scenes of warfare throughout the ages are projected through the blue window of the cell, with the window expanding to movie-screen size.

As the final soldiers pass, the HERMAPHRODITE rises from YUMI'S cot and joins the line: a nude, ludicrous addition to this pageant of force—an absurd exclamation point.

(This display of soldiers should be almost tedious in its presentation, but overwhelming by virtue of its grossness.)

After the parade has passed, the window shrinks to its normal size, and YUMI rises.

YUMI

Here where the rain never stops
life is simple
One can only summon death
not stop it
Relieve yourself of the effort
before it becomes
absolutely necessary
What the sky says
I remember

The noise beyond my ears
is outrageous—
Do you see the bird
the pattern in the mud
People disappear
before they pass
the body is forgotten
a horse in the fog
darkness is certain
laughter is incomplete
the clown amuses himself
waves freeze
postcards of the unreal
false messages
cheap apples
a boy behind the curtain
big hands
horns for the dead
everyone wears a hat
love is a response
religion is the river
all men are lonely
one look says it all
faces pass the rest comes later
it's certainly peaceful
in the country
don't take my picture
the man still can't answer
it's over for the cowboy

the brain is responsible
careful of a smile
portrait of a dog
wrinkles in the air
a dreadful idea and more
writing with lipstick is sick
don't harm the reflection
paint wings on everyone
the light is awful
writing on the mirror
being blind is horrible
very few objects are left
don't be there
do you see the bird yet—
Friends come and go
so few true
only rain returns
year after year
how many faces
disappear—
raindrops

End of The Dreams (Part Five)

Madrugada

(Goes from just before dawn to light)

YUMI is adrift on the raft. Waves rise and crash, threatening to swamp the flimsy craft. Suddenly, the raft is lifted from the sea. It splinters and falls away as a giant WHALE emerges from the water with YUMI riding on its back. At that moment, dozens of other WHALES surface, accompanying the first whale that carries YUMI. The school of whales lifts the stage and ascends over the audience. The whales sing as they fly, rising and dipping as if they were swimming in the ocean.

ONSTAGE, citizens gather. Foremost among them are LÁGRIMAS, TEVA, ROJO, VERA, POLICEMEN, and PRISON GUARDS. All of the people are astounded by the sight. The cast stands revealed in full light for the first time.

CODA—The Memory of Love

Only the HERMAPHRODITE is onstage.

           HERMAPHRODITE
Remember! The memory of love
is the saving grace
of the human race.
Of course, I know more than you'll ever forget
Or have I forgotten more
Than you know yet?
O well, I don't remember
what I've forgot,
so I'll just say,
forget me not!

FIN